BRIDEGROOM MYSTERION

LEGAE ✝ NOMATAMSANQA SEBAKWANE

Bridegroom Mysterion
by Legae & Nomatamsanqa Sebakwane

Published by Seraph Creative in 2026
United States / United Kingdom / South Africa / Australia
www.seraphcreative.org

ISBN 978-1-971498-89-8

ISBN (eBook) 978-1-971498-90-4

BRIDEGROOM MYSTERION

Hebrews 7 : 22 The Mirror

22 Melchizedeck mirrors Christ in the highest office of priesthood mediator between God and mankind. Jesus is now the living proof of God's covenant pledge to benefit mankind in a far better way than under any previous arrangement.

FOREWORD

Because we had to start a new thing for our children to follow, Rethabile and Olebogeng Sebakwane remember and put to application the words of this book in your minds & hearts and add to it the righteous fresh bread that comes from above so that your children can also benefit as you will benefit from our journey of faithfulness in marriage.

INTRODUCTION TO THE COUPLE

Legae Sebakwane is married only to Nomatamsanqa "Tammy" Sebakwane, we are exclusively in a Heterosexual Christ Centered Kingdom Relationship, we are born again believers of Yeshua Hamashiach, our Lord and Saviour.

We believe in the Biblical Worldview and mystery that He was born of a virgin mother and was baptized in water by John the Baptist! He was crucified on the cross for our sins and died! He was raised from the Dead and ascended to be on the right hand of the Father in Heavenly places. He is the High Priest according to the Order of Melchizedek, the Prince of Peace, and King of Peace. Holy Spirit has come down and baptises by Holy Fire whom without, it is impossible to establish a strong Marriage covenant. Yeshua Hamashiach is and maintains to be the Mediator, Advocate between Us and Our Father, Judge and Sovereign Ruler from the uncreated Divine Realms. Through His Divine Blood, we are sons and daughters, a royal priesthood, New Creations through the blood of Christ, which speaks a better covenant than the blood of Abel. We believe that all the stories and people in the bible are true, and the encounters recorded in the Divine book are old and new testimonies of real events that are still prevalent in today's world for us who walk by Faith. The stories in the bible are about a Divine King's love for His Kingdom. Thus, this book is geared for those who seek the Burning Love of YHWH to enhance and transform our matrimony to be a multifaceted instrument in God's hands for His purpose... As for our family, we Love the Lord.....Shalom.

Thank you to our Father, Son, and Holy Spirit, and the Body of

Christ, who is the salt of the Earth and the Light of the world. To all the couples ministries across the globe devoted to keeping the ancient family blueprints alive.

Family is Strength. Thank you to our spiritual parents across the globe who have mentored us, written and recorded our testimonies to help us strengthen our deep roots in Love, which has given birth to Lovelution Global Ministries.

CONTENTS

Chapter 1 -   9
Roots Of Love: The Foundation Of Family Bonds

Chapter 2 -   21
Generations United: The Legacy Of Oneness

Chapter 3 -   31
The Heartbeat Of Home: Nurturing Love In Every Room

Chapter 4 -   39
Weathering The Storms: Strength In Unity

Chapter 5 -   59
Sacred Traditions: The Rituals That Bind Us

Chapter 6 -   83
Unbreakable Threads: Love Across Time And Distance

Chapter 7 -   89
Couples Of The Bible: The Ministry Of Perfection

References   110

About the Authors   111

Seraph Creative   114

CHAPTER 1

ROOTS OF LOVE AND THE
FOUNDATION OF FAMILY BONDS

THE SACRED COVENANT: A
BIBLICAL PERSPECTIVE

In the beginning, when God created the heavens and the earth, He also laid down the foundation for one of the most profound and sacred covenants known to mankind: MARRIAGE. This spiritual molecular bond, between husband and wife, is not merely a social construct, an event we celebrate, but a divine mystery rooted deeply in the very essence of creation. It embodies allegories, an esoteric mystery, and scientific beyond the human mind, such that we are only catching up to the universal precepts of what it really means to be married on a cosmic sphere. The language we use for marriage in modern culture is not to be limited to our earthly perspective, when we look at creation, we can see the pattern of marriage throughout the universe and our planet.

Our prayer through this book is that we can allow ourselves to journey beyond the veil that was torn in the temple when Yeshua Hamashiach died on the cross, we hope to journey together and occupy territories both in the invisible and visible realms within our hearts, adding colour and paint to the parts of our souls that need to reflect much deeper in the roots of Love for our own benefit and society as a whole.

Let us allow ourselves to explore God's Word from a limitless reality filled with hope and dreams. May we invite Holy Spirit, who is our spiritual paint brush, to shine his multi-coloured rainbow and reveal the kingdom of God within us in a tangible way. May we be transfigured into the same image of God and the unconditional love expand within us to make room in the many mansions of Yahweh's ancient Love to heal our families and nations. May we enjoy the journey and God's Light kindle our light in this world in the mighty name of Yeshua Hamashiach, Amen.

2Cor3:18 AMPC

And all of us, as with unveiled face, [because we] continued to behold [in the Word of God] as in a mirror the glory of the Lord, are constantly being transfigured into His very own image in ever increasing splendor and from one degree of glory to another; [for this comes] from the Lord [Who is] the Spirit.

The bible describes marriage as a reflection of the relationship between Christ and the Church—a mystery that transcends time and culture. Throughout the scriptures, we find the stories of couples who embody the sanctity of this union. Adam and Eve, the first couple, teach us about companionship and the importance of unity. Abraham and Sarah reveal the power of faith and perseverance in the face of trials. Isaac and Rebekah demonstrate the beauty of love that is both patient and kind, while Ruth and Boaz show us the rewards of loyalty and commitment.

But perhaps the most significant couple in the Bible is Christ and His Bride, the Church. This traditional union exemplifies the ultimate expression of sacrificial love, where Christ gave Himself for the Church, that she might be pure and holy. This mystery of the Bride and Groom is not just about the love between two people; it is a divine ordinance and covenant that reflects God's eternal plan for humanity.

John 3:29 AMPC

[29] He who has the bride is the bridegroom; but the groomsman who stands by and listens to him rejoices greatly and heartily on account of the bridegroom's voice. This then is my pleasure and joy, and it is now complete.

LEGAE MEETS NOMATAMSANQA "TAMMY'S" BACKSTORY

We met in Pretoria Technikon during our tertiary days, and (Legae) I was visiting a mutual friend, Apollo Zake who ended up introducing us to each other. This was around 23 years ago when she was 19 years and I was 20 years. I knew then when I saw her that she was "The ONE" and I didn't hesitate to tell her that she would be my wife, broke as I was. I didn't know the depth then of what I was talking about but I knew that I knew this was my last ever commitment to anyone on earth.

I had come to a point in my life where I knew deep down that I just didn't see myself exploring the dating scene, I had arrived at my destination. I had found my soul mate. We had similar upbringings which were worlds apart. When we spoke about our upbringings, we learned a lot of the same traits cut across our upbringing.

I had family in the homelands of South Africa in "Bophutatswana", Northwest, and her homelands were in "Transkei", Eastern Cape. We both grew up and had memories to share when we spoke about rural living experiences we related, we had family, and a portion of our lives were spent in the township and suburban life as well. We went to the same type of schools under the apartheid system and transitioned as Millennials into the New South Africa, integrating with multicultural ethnic groups in the then "Model C" schools.

All that time we were walking that path to find each other. This was definitely my "soul mate" and thus we became very good friends. She left for the Eastern Cape, where she found Christ through Uloyiso Community Church. My friend whose name was also Loyiso was a Pastor's Kid and I was surprised that he was also attending that church when he would go back home to visit in East London. I automatically thought it was named after him because his parents were also in leadership there.

I decided to go visit Tammy in East London with another group of my East London-based friends who attended school in Johannesburg and Pretoria. I hitched a ride, excited to go visit East London for the first time on a road trip. I met Tammy's mom and her cute little sister Anga (my sister-in-law-to-be), who was in primary school then. Tammy kept on hinting that something about her had changed, and she was on a spiritual journey, but I couldn't discern exactly what she was all about. She insisted I go with her to church if I am planning to come visit down often because she didn't want to regress in her spiritual walk in Christ.

I felt a bit taken aback and a little offended in a way because I thought I was on a healthy spiritual trajectory myself. She had definitely changed and there was something I couldn't pinpoint about her which made me curious to go and see this church. Prior to my visit, I had been exploring anthropology and spirituality through many mediums from Hare Krishna, Hindu, Rastafarian, African indigenous knowledge systems, Muslim, Black Intelligentsia, New Age, Conscious Hip-Hop, etc. So this was going to be another one of those ordinary events to accompany Tammy to another community church.

After my first visit, I found myself visiting again, and even though they were speaking in Xhosa, which I heard nothing but deep clicks and tongue twisters, I thought they had the best band, which played the best church grooves. I immediately saw that I could do hip-hop and rap with that band. With no filters for protocol, I carried with me an old camera so I would take pictures of the church service whilst they were worshiping with their eyes closed, high as a kite from smoking, and intrigued by this group of Pentecostal folk.

They were really accommodating and gracious as they kept it moving and not making me feel unwelcome into their space with my long dreadlocks, as I ponder looking back. After my next few visits, I had my own encounter with Christ at that small church of Uloyiso Community Church, St. Peter's, Southernwood, East London. On a normal day of worship in song, I had my eyes closed like everyone did, as I had observed Tammy and everyone else were doing it, and I didn't want to be left behind in case I was missing out on something. Suddenly, my inner ears opened and whilst my eyes were closed, a bright light shining through the mosaic windows of the church congregation of about 25 people, overwhelmed me with a strong, tangible presence of an outer-world experience.

I heard a Choir singing with my eyes closed, the louder I heard it, the more I shut my eyelids to focus on this ethereal music. The bright white light covered me all over, and I was enveloped in another dimension. When I opened my eyes again, I was at the front of the church accepting Yeshua Hamashiach as my Lord and Saviour with a few other folks. The sound of thousands of voices singing with the 25 congregants in the small church opened my spiritual eyes to a new dimension, which had me undone. This was the most powerful encounter I had, where months earlier I attended a black intelligentsia conference meeting where very respected intellectuals, whom I will not mention by name, were mocking a brave Christian Pastor saying he was a lost cause for believing in this foreign God.

My theoretical and historical Christian worldview of the historical church murders and colonization of indigenous people and apartheid rhetoric, which were valid, were now undone. I had a practical experience and first-hand encounter with God for myself, and that trumped everything I had thought or experienced in my spiritual walk. I was Born Again and yet from that encounter was left with many questions!!

Tammy's encounter with God in East London, Emonti was already moving in leaps and bounds as God had opened a door for her to work, and God's Grace and goodness were the encounter that made her fall in love with God to give her life to Christ. Her career was taking off in a supernatural manner, and the acceleration working at the harbour and continuing her studies made it a no-brainer for her to accept Yeshua Hamashiach as her Lord and saviour. When I visited East London, Emonti again, Advocate Mzie Yawa and Dr. Sibongile Yawa, our pastor, offered to counsel any of the young adult group planning to get married in the future. Although there were many dating behind the scenes in this church, we were oblivious to church do's and don't so "innocently dating". It was official at our homes, the "Model C" kids had nothing to hide, and because we were comfortable with who we were, we had nothing to be ashamed of, right? So, being the modern couple, "free spirited" in the world, we thought we should raise our hands up and get a sneak preview of what "pre-marital counseling" was all about.

This was actually a divinely orchestrated pathway in disguise..... as in The Way, The Truth, and The Life Himself, opening The Door for us to step into the ancient pathways. Now I perceive it this way, but then we were curious, young lovers who said let's understand deeper what I had said to Tammy when I first met her at first sight many moons ago in Pretoria Technikon. Our behaviour in the church then in Easter Cape was "unheard of", we pushed the boundaries unawares and we would be holding hands and sometimes cuddling during the service.

It was through marriage counseling that we were taught the

boundaries of living in Christ as singles, and we began to practice the hands-free approach in the church walls. We even went to the point that we were told to stop being intimate, and we held our horses if we were planning to spend the rest of our lives. We both thought that's proper and makes absolute sense. We both came from traditional churches, mine being Catholic and hers Anglican.

We were integrated into the new South Africa after 1994. We were exposed to our single parents, who watched local and international soapies like Generations and The Bold and the Beautiful, TV content like The Wonder Years on KTV's MNET, and taught us about how girlfriends and boyfriends relate. We saw how cool musicians were on SABC TV Shows like JAM ALLEY. So media culture from the West influenced our behaviour, and yes, we were young and expressed the progression of culture and the times.

Uloyiso Community Church was established to support students studying in the city with a spiritual home away from home and instill solid foundations of loving families in the future with biblical sound principles. It was a voluntary church, and our pastors were full-time employed in the marketplace, they were just an extended family for young adults who needed some love and questions answered in a world of broken families. That was our sign of miracles and wonders, they didn't have to do any of what they did according to the order of the day, but they intentionally did it anyway. There are a plethora of successful C-Suite leaders out there traveling across the world with no care for our community because our work environments are strenuous and tough, but these guys were flowing in a different type of supernatural, purposeful, quiet fire of the Holy Spirit, which was infectious. Many pastors around were even heard to have made rumours about our church to be likened to a creche experiment.

I don't blame them with youth like us attending there, it would not be appealing to people with traditional backgrounds from church history of Basilica temple structures that serve as historical sites. This was something fresh, fun, and something new. Looking back, I just see God's Love shining on us through that ministry. God's reason why some churches are established is to accommodate and mend broken wings of youth like us, "Free Radicals" in order to shape them to transform the world around them for a greater good.

Fast forward, we are in the middle of our counseling session, and we are no longer intimate, which is good. We find out months later Tammy has conceived, I don't believe I was going to have handled it well if I had not encountered Christ early on. There was a peace in my heart as young as I was that God was going to see me through this new adventure ahead. I was going to do the right thing, and we agreed that we would get married before our boy is born. We would have to move the wedding from next year to a few months before. Advocate e and Dr. Sibongile Yawa had done a work in our hearts to reveal to us the difference between a Covenant Marriage and Contractual Marriage. A Covenant Marriage is a Divine Marriage between God, Husband, and Wife, which means the bond of a Covenant is unbreakable but a contractual marriage can be broken. Thus, a Covenant Marriage is a Love with a Foundation of Unconditional Love, and a contractual marriage is based on conditional love. We will unpack this further in chapters to come.

This Covenant Marriage was the revelation and God's guarantee to us that if we continue to grow in Love with Him, we will be Okay. No matter what happens:

I Corinthians 13:8 NIV

GOD's LOVE NEVER FAILS.

My Father spoke to my late father-in-law and with our pastors to debrief on our behalf what was going on between us and our stance to be responsible and have our wedding before our children were born. Tammy was moved to Daniel fast and pray for 30 days whilst pregnant and to see God's supernatural favor over all the logistics of both our divorced parents coming to witness our wedding matrimony come to pass.

This was a miracle because the Unity and support of our family and church gave us, was beyond this world. Would we do it like this again? The sex before marriage and all? Of course, we would teach what we teach to our children now, hold your horses, and plan better for your family. For us, it has been imperative that we become scholars of the Word of God because we had both come from broken families. It was an uphill for our parents to comprehend so quickly that they were now becoming grandparents so early and we understood our reluctance for us being married by the gravitational pull of seeing their young kids start a family on the back-burner of our traumas. 19 years later in our walk of Faith in Christ the scripture verse:

Romans 8:28 NIV

"And we know that in all things God works for the good of those who love him, who have been called according to his purpose." has a deeper meaning now than when we started.

My father got remarried and is still married today, which is a blessing from God. From our first month of being married, we were thrown into the deep end by our spiritual mentors, Apostle Simphiwe and Pst. Thabsile Kondlo, alongside the couple who walked with us during pre-marital counseling, Advocate Mzie Yawa and Dr. Sibongile Yawa. They invited us into a combined couples fellowship with various pastors, as we were at the tender ages of 24 and 23 years old. Then it was just us and another couple who were fresh from the box, as the first couple to be married in our church. We are still married even today which is such a blessing from God. We were exposed early to the challenges the married pastors were facing and also learned how they are weathering the highs and lows of our journey.

Although we were a tinge overwhelmed by their journeys, we were comforted to connect with more married couples around the city, and also found some who were similar to us from different cultural backgrounds. We went around visiting more couples and were intentional about learning from them how to establish our rhythm as a young married couple.

REFLECTION EXERCISE FOR COUPLES:

1. Reflect on Shared Values & Spiritual Priorities

Focus: Understanding what united us spiritually and how it shaped our commitment.

- What aspects of our faith (e.g., scripture, prayer, church community) were most important to us as a couple in the early stages?
- How did our shared beliefs about God's purpose for marriage influence our decision to commit to one another?
- Were there areas where we disagreed spiritually at the start? How did we resolve or grow in those areas?

2. Assess our Spiritual Foundation-Building Plan

Focus: How intentionally did we cultivate a Christ-centered partnership?

- How did we establish spiritual rhythms together (e.g., praying, attending church, studying the Bible) before or early in marriage?
- Did we discuss long-term spiritual goals (e.g., raising children in the faith, serving in ministry, financial stewardship)? How have these evolved?
- How did we navigate differences in spiritual maturity, denominational backgrounds, or worship styles initially?

3. Evaluate Pre-Marital Counseling Experiences

Focus: The role of guidance in preparing for a lifelong covenant.

- Did we participate in pre-marital counseling (Christian or secular)? What key lessons did we take from it?
- Which tools or discussions from counseling (e.g., conflict resolution strategies, financial planning, expectations about roles) have been most valuable in our marriage?
- Is there an area we should've explored more deeply during counseling (e.g., sex, extended family dynamics, spiritual unity)?

4. Explore Communication & Conflict Resolution Roots

Focus: How faith shaped our approach to unity and disagreement.

- Early on, how did we handle conflicts? Did we rely on biblical principles like forgiveness (Colossians 3:13) or peacemaking (Matthew 5:9)?
- Were there moments in our engagement or early marriage where we felt God guided our communication?
- How has our approach to resolving disagreements grown since our foundation phase?

5. Gauge Preparedness & Lessons Learned

Focus: Honesty about readiness for lifelong union and growth.

- Looking back, what did we feel most prepared for spiritually, emotionally, or practically before marriage?
- What surprised us about married life that we hadn't anticipated during the foundation phase?
- How has our understanding of "leaving and cleaving" (Genesis 2:24) evolved since our early days as a couple?

CHAPTER 2

GENERATIONS UNITED AND THE LEGACY OF ONENESS

CULTURE, MEDIA & THE EROSION OF SACRED VALUES

Genesis 1: 27-28 NIV

[27] **So God created man in his own image, in the image of God created he him; male and female created he them. 28 And God blessed them, and God said unto them, Be fruitful, and multiply, and replenish the earth, and subdue it: and have dominion over the fish of the sea, and over the fowl of the air, and over every living thing that moves upon the earth.**

Over time, many of these sacred truths about relationships have been lost or distorted, influenced by culture, media, and the glamorization of love in Hollywood. The concept of marriage as a covenant has been overshadowed by the fleeting ideals of romance and physical attraction. The depth of commitment and significance of marriage are often overlooked in favor of temporary pleasures and superficial connections.

In today's world, where love is often portrayed as a feeling rather than a revelation of the nature and character of God, it is crucial to revisit the biblical foundations of marriage. We must bring back the mystery of Christ as the Husband and the Church as His Wife into today's context. By doing so, we can restore the sacredness of marriage and encourage couples to build our relationships on the solid rock of faith, rather than the shifting sands of modern culture.

When we look into the story of the bible in the book of Genesis, we see that on the sixth day God creates man and woman in our image. (Legae) I have to tell this story because the very basic biology in my timeline is totally different to that of my son's timeline. It was simple to speak of Heterosexual marriage and the natural family, now it has become important that what we term natural science must also be interpreted with natural signs. As a Millennial in South Africa, it is naive to think that the concept of marriage has not been more complex in this generation than any other. I implore you that I still get shocked with how things have panned out, and the reasons why some marriages have been torn apart were because of same sex reasons is painful to say the least.

Ephesians 6: 11 AMPC

11Put on God's whole armor [the armor of a heavy-armed soldier which God supplies], that you may be able successfully to stand up against [all] the strategies and the deceits of the devil.

When we got married, we didn't exactly realise that we had just secured ourselves a spot in God's Army, we had enrolled into an ancient spiritual war taking place silently amongst our families and greater society. As we interacted with more people, we also came across our peers who got divorced early on in the journey and had developed empathy for them. Especially for those who had children because we knew firsthand what it is like to live in a broken home. The more we engaged with more people, the more we realised a pattern and the variable reasons why they got divorced helped us to grow in the gift of discernment between spirits, in understanding and wisdom. A real daily battle was unfolding before us, and it was never going to be business as usual. A week before Tammy's water broke, she was fired at work, to make things extra spicy and easy for our journey ahead, right?

We can laugh now but then we experienced mixed feelings, a warning shot with the aim to hurt our marriage and unborn child from financial stress and so forth. But the Grace of God was with us in every step. Our covering spiritually at Uloyiso Community Church again was at our rescue. We were living in one of our leaders flat But Thami for free until we got on our feet, bless his heart.....he literally handed over the place fully furnished and would come there only when he was in East London occasionally, as he had another base in Kwa-Zulu Natal and traveled a lot with work.

Tammy got another job and for a season, I was looking after our little baby boy. It was no easy job at the beginning phase. I was this young fellow, married and tagging along with my son everywhere I went, strapped to a kangaroo, be it a business meeting, the grocery store or the bank. It was unusual and unheard of in a Xhosa, staunch East London culture but I got around well. In South African culture, it is said "uchatiwe" or "o nyetswe" which means " you are supposed to be living where you came from and take your wife with you when you get married. A cleave and leave type of situation. Well.......God had also given us wisdom to grow our roots in our spiritual family church and learn through the Couples Fellowship post-marital workshops they hosted, what it means to live out life in marriage with Christ.

We grew from strength to strength exponentially, spending time with Prof. Ntintili and Pst. Mlungwana Senior, who were raising their own children in our age group under the banner of Christ. We drank from their well and were immensely equipped for the battle ahead. It was through them that we came across the book No More Two by Gbile Akanni. It was in this period where we were exposed to the message of oneness, as we term it. We collected a library of books from seasoned marriage ministry authors like Gary Chapman and James C. Dobson. We were subscribed to a Continuous Education Programme from Network 21 with John Maxwell, and a range of books through our network marketing business we were involved in.

We attended these network marketing seminars where couples were building global businesses successfully and had a bigger outlook of marriage on a global scale, ideas such as generational wealth were unfolding before us, and we felt God had a bigger plan for marriage beyond our wildest dreams. When TD Jakes and the late Pst. Myles Munroe came to South Africa. We were fortunate to attend Trinity Broadcasting Network Africa in East London, to reinforce ourselves. We became students of this institution of God, and for five years, we incubated ourselves in this process nonstop.

We also learned that the first five years of marriage were tough, we saw that many younger couples who dropped out and divorced had not fully understood the ancient spiritual war as we saw it. The reasons some of them were leaving each other very early off the bat were petty things that were superficial. It had dawned to us that without a spiritual encounter with God, it was never going to be perceived as a sacred institution in this journey of marriage.

Proverbs 24: 6 TLV

For with wise advice you wage war and in many counselors there is victory

Some of them were valid reasons of domestic violence, substance abuse, and infidelity. On the other hand, we also met those who were willing to hold on and turn things around to make their marriage work. Daily we begin to learn that when you get closer and peer into our reasons for leaving, the pattern is always one of the three: pride of life, lust of the flesh, or lust of the eyes. In modern terms, this is another way of saying being selfish to the extent that a compromise will not be made because one party wants to be more righteous than the other. This is the basis and focus of the contractual marriage paradigm instead of the Covenant Marriage.

We had thought that everyone who was married in our interactions with couples from other ministries that we met, who believed in Christ, had gone through pre-marital counseling and were attending post marital counseling sessions like us at Uloyiso Community Church, but yet again we were young and naive. We stayed there until we were ten years in marriage, and God released us to come up to Gauteng to be closer to my side of the family in Gauteng.

Nineteen Years later, in July 2025, we are still unlearning and learning what we used to think was marriage and what it is in this season of our lives.

A PERSONAL JOURNEY: THE EARLY DAYS OF OUR MARRIAGE

In the early days of our marriage, we were full of hope and excitement, eager to build a life together. But like all couples, we faced our share of challenges. There were moments of joy, but also times of struggle. We learned that marriage is not always easy, but it is always worth the effort.

One of the most significant lessons we learned was the importance of communication. In those early days, we often found ourselves talking past each other, assuming that the other person understood our thoughts and feelings. It took time, patience, and a lot of prayer to develop the kind of open, honest communication that is the bedrock of a strong marriage.

We also discovered the value of laughter. In the midst of stress and uncertainty, we learned to find joy in the little things. Whether it was a shared joke or a spontaneous dance in the living room, these moments of light-heartedness brought us closer together and reminded us of the love that first brought us together.

As we look back on those early days, we are grateful for the lessons we learned and the foundation we built. Our marriage is perfect in Christ, and it is rooted in Love. A love that has grown stronger with each passing day, nourished by faith, commitment, and the grace of God.

This first chapter sets the stage for the journey that lies ahead, exploring the deep roots of love that form the foundation of family bonds. Through the lens of scripture, practical advice, and personal testimony, we will delve into the heart of what makes a marriage strong, enduring, and, above all, sacred.

The early days of marriage are a time of discovery, where the merging of two lives into one begins. For us, the concept of oneness was now just a lifestyle, a practical foundation that would define our union and shield it from the fractures of our past. Both of us had come a long way from undoing traumas from homes where divorce had torn our families apart, leaving deep scars and unanswered questions about the nature of love and commitment.

However, as we embarked on our journey together, we found ourselves drawn to the profound lessons in the book "No - More - Two" by Pastor Gbile Akanni — a book that would shape our understanding of what it truly means to become one in marriage.

Pastor Akanni's book presents a powerful image of the first marriage, one that predates any human tradition or culture. It begins with Adam, a man created whole, but destined for something greater. God, in His wisdom, did not create Eve as a separate being from the start. Instead, He took Eve from Adam, splitting him in a way that made them two whole new beings from one whole—like an atom divided, each part carrying the essence of the other.

Eve, the perfect mirror image of Adam's feminine self, was not just a companion, but a fully-fledged soul that emanated from a piece of him — a reflection of his own soul in another form. This imagery resonated deeply with us, this formed another building block to the Covenant Marriage revelation we got from our mentors.

God revealed that marriage was not about two individuals living alongside each other, but about becoming one entity, united in purpose, vision, and love for God and each other.

It was a revelation that redefined our approach to our relationship, shifting our focus from individuality to another deeper level of unity. One of the key lessons from "No More Two" that stood out to us was the revelation that when God created Eve from Adam, He was establishing a divine order for marriage — a pattern of unity and interdependence. This was not just a physical or emotional bond, but a sacred fusion where the strengths and weaknesses of each partner were balanced by the other. In this light, marriage was not about finding someone to complete you, but about recognizing that you are already one—two individual wholes which make a divine whole. One plus one is equal to one in marriage mathematics.

To internalize this concept of ONENESS, we also began to engage in practical activities designed to strengthen our unity. We realized that oneness in marriage was something that had to be cultivated intentionally, not just assumed because we had exchanged vows. We started with simple daily practices—things like praying together each morning, sharing a meal without distractions, and setting aside time each week for deep, honest conversations. It was no easy task as we were also child-rearing from the get-go. Night times were for changing diapers and feeding our baby whilst Tammy caught up with her sleep to recharge and find rest.

These activities were dynamic and also new territories to navigate for a season. When we got into a rhythm, we continued to focus on aligning our hearts and minds, ensuring that we were moving in the same direction in every area of our lives.

One of our favorite things to do was what we called "vision sharing or dream building." For a minimum of once a week per month, we would sit down together and talk about our dreams, goals, and the vision we had for our future as a couple. This exercise was not just about setting goals, but about making sure that we were both on the same page, that our individual desires were harmonized into a shared vision. It was during these sessions that we discovered the power of unity in decision-making. Rather than making decisions independently and then informing each other, we learned to make decisions together, ensuring that every step we took was a step taken as one.

As we navigated the early years of our marriage, we found ourselves often reflecting on our personal testimonies. We were feeding off each other's strength through Christ and from the stories of overcoming from couples making progress around us. Coming from divorced families, we had seen firsthand the pain and destruction that could come from a lack of unity. But rather than allowing this to cast a shadow over our marriage, we chose to see it as a motivation, a reason to fight even harder for our oneness.

We knew that if we grasped the concept of oneness, divorce would not be an option. For us, marriage was not just a partnership, but a merger — two lives fused into one, with no room for blame or division.

Ephesians 4: 26-27 NIV

[26] "Be angry, yet do not sin. Do not let the sun go down on your anger, [27] nor give the devil a foothold."

In moments of conflict, which inevitably arose, we remembered the lessons from "No More Two." Rather than pointing fingers or assigning blame, we reminded ourselves that we were not two individuals in opposition, but one united front. Our fights were not battles to be won or lost, but opportunities to grow together, to strengthen the bond that made us one. Each disagreement was a chance to learn more about each other, to understand our weaknesses, and to find ways to support each other better.

In the midst of all this, we realized a profound truth: oneness in marriage is not a destination, but a journey. It is something that must be pursued daily, nurtured through intentional actions and attitudes. It is about choosing to be united even when it would be easier to stand apart. It is about recognizing that in marriage, there is no "I" or "you," only "us and we."

Our story is a testament to the power of oneness — a legacy that we hope to pass on to future generations. We have learned that when two people truly become one, marriage becomes an unbreakable bond, a reflection of the divine unity that God intended from the beginning. And as we continue to grow together, we are committed to living out this legacy, ensuring that our oneness is not just a concept, but a reality that shapes every aspect of our lives.

As we look to the future, we do so with the knowledge that our marriage is built on a solid foundation—a foundation that will stand the test of time, because it is rooted in the divine order of oneness that God Himself established. And in this oneness, we find the strength, the joy, and the love that make our marriage not just a union of two people, but a reflection of something far greater.

PRACTICAL APPLICATIONS: STRENGTHEN THE BOND

For newlyweds and those preparing for marriage, it is essential to engage in activities that strengthen the bond between husband and wife. Here are some practical ideas:

1. Prayer and Devotion: Begin each day with prayer and devotion, inviting God into your relationship. This practice not only strengthens your spiritual bond but also fosters communication and mutual understanding.

2. Study the Word Together: Dive into the scriptures as a couple, exploring the biblical principles of marriage. Discuss what

you learn and how you can apply these teachings to your daily lives.

3. Regular Date Nights: Set aside time each week for a date night. Whether it's a fancy dinner or a simple walk in the park, the key is to spend quality time together, away from the distractions of daily life.

4. Service Projects: Participate in service projects together. Serving others as a team helps build a sense of purpose and unity in your marriage.

5. Marriage Retreats: Consider attending a marriage retreat or seminar. These events offer valuable insights and tools for strengthening your relationship.

CHAPTER 3

THE HEARTBEAT OF OUR HOME

NURTURING LOVE IN EVERY ROOM

In the quiet moments of reflection, Legae and Tammy often found themselves contemplating the words of John 14:1-3, where Jesus spoke of preparing a place for His followers in His Father's house. This scripture was more than a promise of an eternal home; it was a blueprint for how we could structure our own home on earth — a home where love, integrity, and faith were the foundation of every room. We learned early on from our Apostles and marriage mentors, Simphiwe and Thabsile Kondlo, that true integrity comes when we integrate God into every area of our lives. For them, this meant creating a home where God's presence was not confined to just one room or aspect of our lives, but infused into every corner and decision we made.

From the beginning, we were intentional about making our home a place where love could flourish, where every room had a purpose that went beyond its physical function. We envisioned our home not just as a shelter but as a sanctuary — a place where God's love could be felt in every conversation, every action, and every interaction. It was a place where we could nurture our marriage, raise our children, and build a life that reflected the values we held dear.

One of the key lessons we embraced was the importance of integrating God into our everyday activities. Whether it was in our business, our health and wellness, our community involvement, or our creative endeavors, we understood that making room for God meant more than just praying or reading the Bible. It meant inviting His presence into every decision, every plan, and every aspiration. It was about ensuring that our home was a place where God's love was evident in everything we did.

PRACTICAL WAYS TO NURTURE LOVE IN EVERY ROOM

In our journey of creating a Christ - centered home, we developed several practical activities to ensure that love and unity were nurtured in every room. These activities were simple yet profound, designed to bring us closer together as a couple, strengthen our family bonds, and keep our home aligned with our family values.

Proverbs 24: 3-4 NIV

[3] By wisdom a house is built, by understanding it is prepared, [4] and by knowledge its rooms are filled with every rare and pleasing treasure.

1. The Living Room: Creating a Space for Reflection and Connection

The living room was more than just a place to relax; it was the heartbeat of our home, where family members gathered to connect and share our lives. To nurture love in this space, we occasionally established "Family Reflection Night." Between Friday and Sunday evening, we would gather in the living room to discuss the highs and lows of the week, share what we were grateful for, and reflect on a scripture that spoke to our current season of life. This practice not only deepened our connection with each other but also helped us stay grounded in our faith, reminding us of God's presence in our daily lives. We also made sure that for the first 5 years, we don't get a TV in the house, so that we are always engaging with each other and have no external media content working against our values. We curated content for our children where we had Christian Cartoons sourced from local and international book stores, and for us from Gospel House Music, Gospel Hip-hop, Gospel Kwaito, Gospel Reggae, Gospel Dancehall, Gospel Rock and Gospel Jazz.

2. The Kitchen: Cooking with Love and Intention

The kitchen is where nourishment for the body and soul begins. We discovered that cooking occasionally together was a powerful way to nurture our relationship. We turned meal preparation into a bonding activity, where we could experiment with new recipes, pray over the food we prepared, and discuss the blessings of the day. We also made a point of involving our children, teaching them the importance of gratitude and service as we prepared meals together. By transforming cooking into a shared act of love, we reinforced the idea that our home was a place where everyone contributed to the well-being of the family. As our children got older in high school, we continued to intentionally involve them as they grew to have more responsibilities with homework and school sports. On weekends, we would occasionally task them to take over the cooking and washing of dishes.

3. The Bedroom: Cultivating Intimacy and Rest

The bedroom is our sanctuary, a place of rest, intimacy, and rejuvenation. To nurture love in this space, we created a nightly new tradition we called "The Gratitude Exchange." Before going to sleep, we would share something we were thankful for about the other person — whether it was a kind gesture, a word of encouragement, or simply the way we supported each other through the day. That's a Fire Starter! Early in the morning, at 4am we have devotions. This simple practice helped us end each day on a positive note, reinforcing our love and appreciation for one another.

4. The Home Office: Integrating God into Our Vocation

As entrepreneurs who run a family business, the home office is a significant space where we spend a lot of time. To ensure that this room also reflected our commitment to a Christ - centered life, we dedicated the first 15 minutes of each workday to prayer and reflection. We would pray over our business decisions, ask for God's guidance in our work, and seek His wisdom in the challenges we faced. This practice reminded us that our work was not just about making a living, but about fulfilling our calling to serve others and build God's Kingdom through our business.

5. The Children's Room: Instilling Faith and Values

For our family, nurturing love in our children's room meant creating an environment where our kids could grow in faith and character. We established a bedtime routine that included reading Bible stories, praying together, and discussing the lessons we could apply in our lives. We also encouraged our children to keep a "Blessings Journal," where we could write down or draw pictures of the things we were thankful for weekly. This not only helped our children develop a habit of gratitude but also reinforced the idea that our home was a place where God's love was always present.

INTEGRATING GOD IN EVERY ASPECT OF LIFE

Our commitment to integrating God into every room of our home extended beyond physical spaces. We believed that to truly nurture love and integrity, we needed to make room for God in every aspect of our lives. This holistic approach to spirituality meant that we sought to bring God's presence into our business, our health, our creative projects, and our community involvement.

1. In Business: We founded a family business together, with the conviction that our work should reflect our values and serve a higher purpose. We took courses together to better ourselves, constantly seeking ways to improve and grow. We saw our business not just as a means of income but as a ministry — an opportunity to bless others and spread the love of Christ through our work.

2. In Health and Wellness: Recognizing that our bodies were temples of the Holy Spirit, we made a conscious effort to involve God in our health and wellness journey. We fast and pray for strength and discipline in our exercise routines, making healthy eating choices, and encouraging each other to stay active. By making God a part of our health goals, we found motivation and accountability in each other, ensuring that we remained strong and vibrant for the journey ahead.

3. In Community Service: Whenever opportunities arise to serve in church, NPOs, globally funded community development or government spheres, we see it as a chance to extend God's love beyond the walls of our home. Whether through volunteering, mentoring, or participating in local initiatives, we sought to be a light in our community, demonstrating the love of Christ through our actions.

4. In Creativity: As creative individuals, we are passionate about using our talents to glorify God. We often get spiritual downloads and blueprints to work and implement on projects to the Glory

of God. Whether through the arts, sports, or media, we dedicated our creative projects to spreading messages of hope, love, and faith.

We collected, created, published and distributed Christ-centered merchandise and media content, ensuring that everything we produced reflected the values we held dear.

A WHOLISTIC APPROACH TO BUILDING GOD'S KINGDOM

Through our journey, we developed a holistic approach — a blueprint for building God's Kingdom that encompassed every area of our lives. We understood that nurturing love in our home was not just about creating a peaceful and happy environment, but about ensuring that our lives were fully aligned with God's will. By making room for God in every room of our home and every aspect of our lives, we created a legacy of love, integrity, and faith that would impact generations to come.

As we continue to walk this path, we remain committed to nurturing love in every room of our home, integrating God into every decision we make, and living out the values we hold dear. Our home is not just a place of shelter, but a sanctuary — a reflection of the eternal home that Jesus has prepared for us, where love, faith, and integrity are the heartbeat of every room. Example Activity: "Love Letters in Every Room"

To nurture love in every room of your home, try this activity called "Love Letters in Every Room." Write short, heartfelt notes to each other via WhatsApp text or Voicenotes throughout the day. These notes/voicenotes could be words of encouragement, expressions of gratitude, or reminders of your love for one another. When you meet, remind each other of these beautiful notes. Over time, as you discover these notes, you'll be reminded of the love that fills every corner of your home. This simple act of leaving love letters for each other is a way to keep the spirit of love alive, making every room in your home a testament to your commitment to each other.

We have learned to discern that God's presence and angels fill every room in our house and our spiritual estate through this Bridegroom Mysterion. Our how is a gateway, an embassy, and earthly host for Jacob's ladder in our community. Cultivating an atmosphere of heaven in our home is a privilege we get to steward in our intimate walk of Faith with Yeshua The Husband of our Marriage Covenant.

CHAPTER 4

WEATHERING THE STORMS

Psalm 107:29 NASB

He caused the storm to be still, So that the waves of the sea were hushed.

When we stood before the altar, hand in hand, we envisioned a future painted with the bright hues of love, laughter, and unshakeable faith. We knew our journey wouldn't always be easy—no marriage ever is—but we hadn't fully grasped just how fierce the storms would be. We believed that love, anchored in faith, would see us through any storm, trial, highs and lows. What we didn't yet realize was that it wasn't just the love that would carry us, but the power of our Covenant Lover, forging our unity and the strength we would draw from our faith in Him as a family.

But life, as it often does, had more in store for us. An example of a storm we faced was with the sudden news of a call that came for me (Legae). (Legae) My father had suffered a severe stroke, leaving him partially paralyzed and unable to speak. The weight of responsibility pressed down on me, as I tried to balance being there for my father, on our arrival to see my father.....I (Tammy) received a call that shattered my world. My father, who had always been a rock in my life, had passed away unexpectedly. The grief was overwhelming, a wave that threatened to drown me. As I clung to Legae, my tears soaking his shirt, I felt as though a piece of my heart had been ripped away. Legae, though struggling with his own emotions, knew he had to be strong for me. That very day, I (Legae) whispered prayers into the night, asking for strength to support my wife through this loss. Supporting Tammy in her grief and managing our own household, needed me to tap into the supernatural Grace of God to overcome. The days blurred together, we had to leave my father and go home, one thousand five hundred kilometers across South Africa, to mourn and bury Tammy's father.

It seemed as though the very ground beneath us was shifting, unsteady and unpredictable. But we knew we couldn't afford to be swept away by the chaos. We had to stand firm, not only for ourselves but for our young sons, Olebogeng and Rethabile, who were barely old enough to understand the changes in our once-happy home.

Just when we thought we had weathered the worst of the storms, a few years later, Olebogeng fell gravely ill. His condition baffled medical doctors, and their medicine offered no relief. We felt as though we were being tested beyond our limits. But in this darkest hour, we found hope in an unexpected place. A close friend suggested we try a natural homeopathic treatment, a path we had never considered before to heal a severe disease using organic supplements. With the support of friends who rallied around us, offering both prayers and financial help, we were able to afford the organic supplements Olebogeng needed over a long period.

Days turned into nights as we watched over our son, praying fervently for his recovery. Slowly and miraculously, the treatment began to work. The disease broke, and Olebogeng's strength returned. The storm that had threatened to take our child began to subside, leaving behind a profound sense of gratitude and renewed faith. I (Legae) would lie prostrate on the floor, face down, praying all night for my son's health for weeks on end, sobbing and contending with God to give us authority over this sickness, and we eventually got a breakthrough.

But even as the storm over our son began to calm, another was brewing on the horizon. Family dynamics, always complex, became even more strained as we navigated the traditional expectations of our in-laws from both sides. The biggest contradictions against our faith in Christ were tested whenever there were traditional events. This meant we would attend but choose to be bystanders rather than participate in ancient rituals that would compromise our walk of Faith in Christ. It would come as a shock or even offend some family members, but we stood our ground and maintained our Peace.

A deep revelation of our Marriage Covenant with the Blood of the Lamb has proven to be sufficient and any other sacrifice would be leading to repercussions that our children would have to deal with despite them not participating. The ultimate price has been paid already by Christ and our desire to stay married to Christ as our only God is consistent with our commitment to each other, to build a marriage based on mutual respect and what we believed was righteous before God. Tension was ever palpable, with some family gatherings feeling like a battlefield whenever we met. There were arguments about customs, heated discussions about what was "proper," and the ever-present pressure to conform to traditions that didn't resonate with us.

There was another season when things went south, where we were living on a smallholding in Leeuwfontein, Pretoria North. We were sleeping at night and suddenly Tammy sees a person in our bedroom tiptoeing. She screams out loud and when I wake up, the guy wearing black all over steals our laptop playing in our room and runs for it. (Legae) I chased him with adrenaline flowing in my body, but as he disappeared beyond the floodlights, I heard Holy Spirit say to me let him go. When I went back into the house, we found that my studio film gear, with a TV Show and business hard drives, were looted alongside furniture on the other wing of the house.

The traumatic experience took a couple of months to overcome, and God invited us higher into the supernatural to shift spiritual realms of engagement in Gauteng because the territory spiritually needed us to make an upgrade in order to settle well. It is here when more mysteries of the Bridegroom were activated and God began to open up ministries that walked in authority behind the veil on a new dimension.

> **Ephesians 6:12 <u>TLB</u>**
>
> **For we are not fighting against people made of flesh and blood, but against persons without bodies— the evil rulers of the unseen world, those mighty satanic beings and great evil princes of darkness who rule this world; and against huge numbers of wicked spirits in the spirit world.**

During this season of tantamount difficulties, we remembered the words from:

> **Proverbs 18:10 AMPC**
>
> **The name of the LORD is a strong tower; The righteous runs to it and is safe and set on high [far above evil].**

We realized then that the storms we were facing were meant to break us, but God used them to strengthen us. What we cannot overcome can never come under our authority. We needed to stand firm, like eagles soaring through turbulent skies, finding peace in the eye of the storm.

We knew we had to mature quickly, to adapt and learn how to weather these storms together. We began to seek out God's face to help us stay spiritually intimate to strengthen our bond even in the midst of turmoil.

Matthew 8: 23-27 TLV

[23] As He got into the boat, His disciples followed Him. [24] Suddenly a great storm arose on the sea, so that the boat was being covered by the waves. But *Yeshua* kept on sleeping. [25] So they came and woke Him up, saying, "Master, save us! We're perishing!" [26] He said to them, "Why are you afraid, O you of little faith?" Then He got up and rebuked the winds and the sea, and it became totally calm. [27] The men were amazed, saying, "What kind of person is this? Even the winds and the sea obey Him!"

We discovered that simple, intentional actions could make a world of difference:

1. Praying & Fasting Together: Every morning, we would spend time in prayer, not just individually but as a couple. At times, it was difficult because of the external stresses of putting a demand and working to keep us out of this rhythm. As much as we prayed individually at our own pace, we made the effort to pray and eventually enter into a fasted lifestyle. We engaged in regular all night prayers. Often went into business meetings having prayed and fasted. We prayed for wisdom, for patience, and for the strength to support each other breakthrough whatever storms came our way.

2. Weekly Check-Ins: We established a routine of weekly check-ins, where we would sit down without distractions and talk about our families progress, our challenges, and our victories. This practice helped us stay connected and avoid misunderstandings that could fester into bigger problems. It was not always easy to do it as sometimes even our energy levels were depleted to even talk after work but we make space for communication and silence the voice of our self-negative talks that naturally creep in to sow division.

3. Date Nights at Home: When our financial situation was tight, going out wasn't always an option. But we found creative ways to

have date nights at home — cooking dinner together, watching a favorite movie, or simply sitting on the porch and talking about our dreams for the future. Catching up on how far we've come and counting our blessings and giving God the glory. Even when we were on a very tight budget we would go to a restaurant and share a plate whilst enjoying each other's company.

4. Support Groups: We continued to reach out to other couples in our church and community who had faced similar challenges. We continue to attend couples enrichment seminars. These support groups become a lifeline, offering both practical advice and emotional support.

5. Coaching: Understanding that sometimes we needed help beyond what we could offer each other, we sought out Coaching. Speaking with married elders helped us navigate the complex emotions and challenges we were facing, provided tools to strengthen our relationship. Being asked difficult questions that we don't get to ask each other for the fear of upsetting our partner can also hinder progress. External help is always valuable, especially to receive help from believers who fear the Lord on these matters because both spiritual and physical blind spots can be discerned.

6. Forgiveness and Grace: We made a conscious effort to practice forgiveness, both towards each other and our extended families. We realized that holding onto grudges only added fuel to the storm, whilst reflecting His Grace and Understanding could bring calm. We were taught that unforgiveness is like drinking poison and expecting the person you're not forgiving to feel the pain.

7. Building Family Traditions: We began to establish new family traditions that blended both the positive aspects of our backgrounds while reflecting our shared values. These traditions helped to solidify our family unit and created a sense of continuity amidst the chaos.

Taking Holy Communion Daily and revelations about the Body and the Blood of Christ took on a new meaning. We weathered the storms of Covid 19 through this Bridegroom Mysterion as Tammy was working in the field at the height of COVID in the hospitals, across the country, selling medical supplies, she came out unscathed by His Grace.

8. Mindfulness and Meditation: Recognizing the toll that stress can take on us, we practice mindfulness and meditation on the Word and Testimonies of God. This practice helps us stay grounded and focused, even when external circumstances are overwhelming. It's so easy to focus on the chaos around the world and blame each other without managing our internal thought patterns, the doom and gloom happening in our cities than to pray and be grateful that God has given us life, shelter, food, work, responsibilities and the Power to show Love to one person at a time daily.

Proverbs 4: 23 TLV

Guard your heart diligently, for from it flow the springs of life.

As we implemented these activities, we found that the storms, while still fierce, became more manageable. We were no longer just reacting to the chaos but proactively strengthening our marriage and our family. The miracles of praying and speaking the word literally over circumstances have mystery and power (government) within it.

Speaking God's Word is literally coding the world from within by declaring it to the chaos without. To conform to the patterns of Heaven on Earth. Holy Spirit in us, who is the authority over the physical realm, spiritual realm, angels, and spirit beings, changes by faith the most complex of chaotic events to tune into Yeshua Hamashiach's spiritual laws and authority as The King of Peace.

Matthew 8: 26 TLV

²⁶ He said to them, "Why are you afraid, O you of little faith?" Then He got up and rebuked the winds and the sea, and it became totally calm. ²⁷ The men were amazed, saying, "What kind of person is this? Even the winds and the sea obey Him!"

We have grown in the mysteries of being a bride of Christ daily, our story changed from the fight or flight of just surviving storms into finding strength in the Unity that bound us together in the heavenly places with Christ on the right hand of the Father. We had faced loss, illness, financial struggles, and family tensions, but through it all, we had each other. And in that bond, we discovered the true power of family — an anchor that held us steady even when the world around us seemed to be falling apart. As the first chapters of our journey came to a close, we knew there would be more storms ahead. But we also knew that together we could face anything. With God as our guide, in a covenant marriage, reflecting face to face as one in the Trinity, aligned in spirit, soul and body, all things are possible in Christ. As unwavering partners, we are daily ready to face whatever challenges life has in store for us. A Unity forged in Peace, that no storm could ever take away.

To weather storms in marriage and family life, as couples, we can further engage in several activities that strengthen our bond and build resilience:

1. Open Communication: We regularly set aside time to talk openly and honestly about our feelings, highs and lows, concerns, and needs. We create a safe space where both of us can express ourselves without being judgmental. There's a difference between being of good judgment and judgmental. Being judgmental is speaking in condemnation of your partner which is mostly projecting the wrong image about each other falsely before God's Light. Being of good judgment is about speaking life and righteousness into each other's lives to bring our intimacy in Christ more deeper and experience more freedom from bondage and sin.

Proverbs 31: 8-9 AMPC

[8] Open your mouth for the dumb [those unable to speak for themselves], for the rights of all who are left desolate *and* defenseless; [9] Open your mouth, judge righteously, and administer justice for the poor and needy.

There is a popular saying where couples say (including believers in general) you can't judge. It has become a cliché part of speech for individuals who don't want to walk the talk and be accountable to each other and above board to the Word of God. We then have to admit with Humility that the source of Holiness is Holy Spirit and without alignment with this Person of the Trinity, it is impossible to judge and discern between pride and Humility. Therefore, the best form of communication to each other is the Word of God spoken in Love and Truth to each other, as God has designed this covenant marriage institution in the same pattern.

2 Timothy 2: 15 AMPC

[15] Study *and* be eager *and* do your utmost to present yourself to God approved (tested by trial), a workman who has no cause to be ashamed, correctly analyzing *and* accurately dividing [rightly handling and skillfully teaching] the Word of Truth.

2. Prayer and Meditation: We incorporate prayer and meditation on the Word and Testimonies of God into our daily routine. As we got rooted into this pattern Holy Spirit has led us to incorporate this into advanced variations because we have graduated into it, becoming a lifestyle. This can help couples center, seek divine guidance, and find peace amidst challenges.

Making time for quiet time to listen to God after prayer is part of meditation. Praying, adding Petitions and Supplicating with the Word. Listening to God in quiet time before and after prayer are both important to transform ourselves from cutting the noise externally (without), and our focus is looking for answers from within. Entering into the presence of God.

Psalm 46:10 AMPC

[10] **Let be *and* be still, and know (recognize and understand) that I am God. I will be exalted among the nations! I will be exalted in the earth!**

Isaiah 30:15 AMPC

[15] **For thus said the Lord God, the Holy One of Israel: In returning [to Me] and resting [in Me] you shall be saved; in quietness and in [trusting] confidence shall be your strength.**

3. Shared Goals and Planning: We work together to set and achieve common goals, whether financial, personal, or relational. This fosters teamwork and ensures that both partners are aligned in our efforts. During the height of lockdown Covid 19, we found out that many couples were fighting and could not bear to stay in each other's presence because that part of their life between 8 to 5 was not a time they used to share together. Most couples who failed to adjust and plan how they would share their living spaces did not see eye to eye and called it quits. For some (8 hrs x 20 days of the month = 160 hrs) is spent away from home.

Over 1 year = 1,920 hours of the day away from each other to work. Over 10 years, that is 19,200 hours spent away from home. Now these couples had to spend a whole year together at home which meant 1,920 hours extra. This partner we professed before the public to live in good and tough times would be in my space for a season, non-stop. That was supposed to be a blessing, an opportunity to reset goals and plan new goals.

But to others, it was a disruptive pattern and they missed out on a beautiful window of rich quality time in God's Presence and themselves. This is when we asked God what we could do about it, then He opened a door online for us to launch Zoom coaching sessions where we share our wisdom and support younger couples needing marriage coaching for a season.

Matthew 7: 7-8 AMPC

[7] Keep on asking and it will be given you;   keep on seeking and you will find;   keep on knocking [reverently] and [the door] will be opened to you. [8] For everyone who keeps on asking receives; and he who keeps on seeking finds; and to him who keeps on knocking, [the door] will be opened.

4. Coaching and Support Groups: We seek out marriage counseling, coaching or joined support groups for couples. Professionals, coupled with Spiritual Guidance or the support of others who have faced similar challenges can provide valuable perspectives and solutions. Most importantly, biblically sound advice is important in our context because all we are sharing is within the framework of Christ the King of Glory. For us, it is simple wisdom, when one needs to improve in guitar skills, we find a tutor, take lessons and then eventually play in a duet and graduate into a band. We don't seek out a boxing tutor to learn how to play a guitar, we will hurt both our marriage and mess up the guitar. The same principle applies, birds of the same feather flock together.

5. Quality Time Together: Make time for activities that you both enjoy and that bring joy to your relationship. This could be as simple as a regular date night, a hobby you both enjoy, or taking short trips together. Gary Chapman has a best seller book called the 5 love languages. One of the languages is quality time, he expresses through his research and divine revelation that some partners feel they are loved more when they can spend time alone with their partner, whilst the other partner would feel loved when they see you do an act of service by serving them with a cup of coffee and cake, etc. Taking time to be in the presence of God brings our marriage into deeper intimacy spiritually which also overflows into each other in abundant Love.

6. Financial Planning: Work together on a budget and financial plan. Being transparent about finances and making joint decisions can help prevent misunderstandings and alleviate stress. As entrepreneurs who have worked across sectors in Public, Private and NGO sectors, being employed and unemployed. All I can say in this area is WORKING PROGRESS!!.

We have been working in this area in great depth learning how to balance walking by faith and meeting monthly overheads. Most of the times working with no budget and planning by faith to see God manifesting what we need. Living on manna has not been easy and God has been beyond faithful. In this area we can advise that couples can work towards multiple income streams to build assets from the onset whilst working in their jobs part time. Lifelong learning on how to be good stewards of finance because this will position our marriages to be a blessing to the vast needs in our communities around us. We have had to unlearn Babylon business practices and learn how Our Heavenly Father's Kingdom blueprint for business is supposed to be. It has been our greatest challenge to navigate for many years, a walk of growing in understanding systemic poverty and how spiritual financial altars work.

We have invested in seminars, studied abroad, pitched to financial gurus and high networth individuals to invest in our ideas. We have read financial literacy books, sought help and learned tough lessons getting into bad debts which we are not proud of. Breaking bloodline curses, identity and poverty mindsets to enter His prosperity.

God eventually brought us into kingly anointed alignment with sound biblical kingdom businessmen and women who are walking in His perfect will to help us translate our dreams of prosperity, including financial into fruition and strengthen our net worth to establish His Ecclesia.

We are living in a fallen world and there is much to learn for the body of Christ which altars we trade on and how to align ourselves to build cross-generational kingdom businesses and wealth that is birthed from the third heaven to establish what is in Heaven on Earth.

Psalm 118: 25 – 26 NJKV

25 Save now, I pray, O LORD; O LORD, I pray, send now prosperity. 26 Blessed *is* he who comes in the name of the LORD! We have blessed you from the house of the LORD.

3 John 1: 2 - 3 NJKV

2 Beloved, I pray that you may prosper in all things and be in health, just as your soul prospers. 3 For I rejoiced greatly when brethren came and testified of the truth *that is* in you, just as you walk in the truth.

Deuteronomy 8:18 NJKV

"But you shall remember the LORD your God, for it is He who gives you power to get wealth; that He may establish His covenant which He swore to your fathers, as at this day."

7. Conflict Resolution Skills: We have to take ownership in developing mediation skills for resolving conflicts constructively. This includes active listening, empathy, and finding compromises that respect both partners' perspectives. The most difficult of the 9 fruits of the Spirit, besides Love, Peace, and Joy to cultivate is patience, long suffering, and self-control. It is because these deal with letting go of the part of ourselves which needs to feel, and putting ourselves in other people's shoes.

Yeshua Hamashiach has been a Master at putting himself in everyone's shoes to the highest level by absorbing all our curses of sin and bondage to the tasting of death. All types of demons that can torment a human being, all types of sicknesses, all verbal and physical abuse, iniquity of our forefathers, all the way to Cain killing

Abel, the earth drinking unrighteous blood of murder for the first time in creation and Adam experiencing fear of separation....He tasted all unto death. Was Yeshua Hamashiach patient? Was Yeshua Hamashiach long-suffering?

Was Yeshua Hamashiach exercising self-control? Even though it went over their heads to fulfill scripture, He said that he could order more than 12 legions of angels, which is about 76 000 angels, to come and destroy the frail human army of the Romans.

Matthew 26: 52 NKJV

52 But Jesus said to him, "Put your sword in its place, for all who take the sword will perish by the sword. 53 Or do you think that I cannot now pray to My Father, and He will provide Me with more than twelve legions of angels? 54 How then could the Scriptures be fulfilled, that it must happen thus?"

He understood that if He didn't put Himself in our shoes and absorb all darkness unto Himself, including tasting death, then we would not progress as humanity to enter and qualify to become married or reconciled to Him as New Creations. New Creations receive the authority and rights of the Divine Husband that Christ has won for His beloved, including all the rights assigned to Holy Spirit and the gifts of the spirits or angels to break the spiritual slaves from bondage and captivity.

We are not married to a frail Husband in this Covenant Marriage. Christ made a way for His Divine Heavenly Kingdom Relationship to be as it is in Heaven on Earth forever and ever. This is another Bridegroom Mystery which makes Marriage so sacred before our Sovereign Father.

2 Corinthians 5: 17 NKJV

17 Therefore, if anyone *is* in Christ, *he is* a new creation; old things have passed away; behold, all things have become new. 18 Now all things *are* of God, who has reconciled us to Himself through Jesus Christ, and

has given us the ministry of reconciliation, [19] that is, that God was in Christ reconciling the world to Himself, not imputing their trespasses to them, and has committed to us the word of reconciliation.

Luke 4: 18 – 19 TLV

The *Ruach Adonai* is on me, because He has anointed me to proclaim Good News to the poor. He has sent me to proclaim release to the captives and recovery of sight to the blind, to set free the oppressed, [19] and to proclaim the year of *Adonai's* favor.

8. Express Appreciation: Regularly express gratitude and appreciation for each other. Acknowledging each other's efforts and qualities helps reinforce positive feelings and strengthens the relationship. There is nothing more invigorating than to hear your partner reinforce you to keep strong and cheer you from your corner.

Whether it's encouraging your spouse to study, applying for a new job, keeping the discipline of working out and eating healthy, saying thank you for receiving a gift and being grateful for the opportunity to give a gift, embracing your partner, etc. We have to be creative and continue to ask the spirit of wisdom how we can improve in expressing appreciation. The moment we lose that rhythm, familiarity and familiar spirits can creep in and undermine the momentum built for over years of walking in love with Christ. Seeing our partner through the eyes of God helps us to keep our living waters fresh, fun and Holy. Thank God for your partner and let us express and magnify to each other the Godly qualities we see manifesting through each other. This is a sacred journey and eternity transcends seasons.

Psalm 107:1 AMPC

[1] **O give thanks to the Lord, for He is good; for His mercy** *and* **loving-kindness endure forever!**

9. Physical and Emotional Support: We are there for each other during tough times. Offering emotional support, understanding, and practical help can make a big difference in navigating challenges together. We have been intentional in building a rhythm of foreplay from the time we wake up and our physical intimacy through the revelation that we have to manage our energy and be available for our children as much as for each other.

Children and work can overtake and drain our reserves if we don't cultivate drinking from God's oasis as a lifestyle. Throughout the day, we deposit into each other positive emotions that kindle our love life with God and each other. Everyday brings with it a variable set of events which can make or break your day. From the moment we wake up to the moment we sleep, how soon we go to bed or how late we go to bed will determine how our energy levels will be the next day.

What we eat, what we consume on media, what we listen to and whom we interact with can enhance or regress the way we will experience God's Love on a daily basis. Thus, we have grown to become sensitive in our surroundings and every aspect of our day because it can turn on or turn off our desire for each other intimately at the end of the day. Creating boundaries and moments throughout the day to keep each other excited about life is both individually and both our responsibility. On tough days, we make sure we take walks at the end of the day. Bathing or showering together must continue and never be taken lightly. Showing affection and working towards communicating your partner's love language speaks volumes. We ask our Creator to constantly reveal our shortcomings by repenting and improving on ourselves. This is a marathon, we take it stride by stride with the aim to finish together every day stronger.

Ephesians 5: 22-26 The Mirror

[22] *(Marriage is a portrait of this mutual yielding to one another.)* **Wives give yourselves fully to your husbands as you would to the Lord.** *(Remember verse 2: love is contagious, not reluctant but extravagant. Sacrificial love pleases God like the sweet aroma of worship.)*[23] **In the same way that Christ gives salvation, security and completeness to the church as the head does to the body, the husband is all of that to his wife.** [24] **The church enjoys the full advantage of the complete package of salvation, by yielding themselves fully to Christ; even so the wife enjoys every benefit her husband represents in her abandonment to him.**

[25] **The husband loving his wife pictures the parallel of Christ loving the church completely, and his unreserved giving of himself to us.**

(This is what marriage is all about; it celebrates love's initiative, whether coming from the husband or the wife. This awakens a different level of commitment beyond any sense of duty or guilt.) [26] **Christ is the voice of God's language, immersed in this conversation, his love words bathe us and remove from us every stain of sin.**

10. Maintaining Faith and Hope: We Lean on our Faith and stay Hopeful, even when things are tough. Trusting in a Divine Higher Power and believing in the strength of our relationship can provide comfort and strength. The beauty in this spirit of wisdom and revelation is that we get to draw from the Kingdom of Love within us and pour out unto each other. So God takes the Glory and we get to enjoy the fruit.

John 15: 1-6 The Mirror

[1] **I Am the Authentic Vine! My Father is the Farmer.** [2] **Every offshoot in Me that does not bear fruit, He lifts up from the ground and fastens it to the stake and every fruit bearing part He dresses in order to maximize its yield.** [3] **Your personal pruning and**

dressing already happened in our conversation; The Word made flesh in my person and language is how the Father prepares and sets you up for fruit bearing. [4] Our seamless union, you in Me and I in you, is pictured in the vine: the shoot cannot bear fruit outside of this union. In its abiding in the vine, fruit happens naturally - as with your abiding in Me. [5] I Am the Vine and you are the branches; it is the one who understands this mutual union that naturally bears much fruit - which is impossible to happen apart from Me. [6] Every area of human life that does not continue to be entwined in this place of seamlessness in Me, was already cast forth where it has withered away and is gathered to be burned as firewood.

Engaging in these activities can help couples build a strong foundation and navigate the storms that life may bring. The Bridegroom Mystery of Marriage is beautiful to observe on a daily basis. When we go to school in the world, we write exams for the grade and get our certificates. In marriage, we receive our graduation gowns and certificates signifying we have passed.

Tetelestai!! Meaning It Is Finished, we are reconciled to our Husband Christ and now we will walk in Eternal Life Today...Now! We walk by Faith, we live in Faithfulness, we reflect heaven's glory as the Light's of the world and thus declare to the kingdom of Darkness Victory!! We hope this mystery magnifies why marriage is under such attack.

Hebrews 11: 1-3 The Mirror

[1]Persuasion confirms confident expectation and proves the unseen world to be more real than the seen. Faith celebrates as certain what hope visualizes as future. (*The shadow no longer substitutes the substance. Jesus is the substance of things hoped for the evidence of everything the Prophets foretold. The unveiling of Christ in human life completes mankind's*

every expectation. Col 1:27.) ²People of previous generations received the testimony of their hope in faith. It was faith that made their hope tangible. *(Only the Messiah can give substance to the Messianic hope. No substitute will suffice!)* ³Faith alone explains what is not apparent to the natural eye; how the ages were perfectly framed by the Word of God.

There are spiritual forces of darkness that want this candlelight to be put out. This union that produces future generations that will be Heavenly representatives on Earth, having dominion and subduing the earth and all of creation are the reason why, without revelation we just don't realise we are daily the banner of spiritual mockery to the devil.

He hates marriage and to see the resurrection Life and Power flowing through Covenant Marriage we have in Him Christ the King of Glory is the last joyful noise he wants to hear irritate him on earth. That is why he designs systemic fear and stress through the demonic to get us to give up on our identity of living a victorious life.

With this spirit of wisdom and revelation, we maintain the supernatural bonds of Faith through the royal blood of the Lamb and walk in eternal hope as our weapon of victorious living, cutting through all the internal lies that we used to believe which ensnared many to keep us in the prisons of fight or flight mode.

Matthew 5:14-15 TLV

¹⁴ You are the light of the world. A city set on a hill cannot be hidden. ¹⁵ Neither do people light a lamp and put it under a basket. Instead, they put it on a lampstand so it gives light to all in the house. ¹⁶ In the same way, let your light shine before men so they may see your good works and glorify your Father in heaven.

2 Corinthians 10: 3-5 The Mirror

[3] The fact that we are living in a physical world in human bodies of flesh does not mean that we engage ourselves in a combat dictated to by the typical "tit-for-tat" strategies of the politics of the day. [4] The dynamic of our strategy is revealed in God's ability to disengage mindsets and perceptions that have held people captive in pseudo fortresses for centuries! [5] Every lofty idea and argument positioned against the knowledge of God is cast down and exposed to be a mere invention of our own imagination. We arrest every thought that could possibly trigger an opposing threat to our redeemed identity and innocence at spear point! The calibre of our weapon is empowered by the revelation of the ultimate consequence of the obedience of Christ.

Ephesians 6:12 TLB

For we are not fighting against people made of flesh and blood, but against persons without bodies— the evil rulers of the unseen world, those mighty satanic beings and great evil princes of darkness who rule this world; and against huge numbers of wicked spirits in the spirit world.

CHAPTER 5

SACRED TRADITIONS AND THE RITUALS THAT BIND US

Colossians 2:8 The Mirror

[8] Make sure that you become no one's victim through empty philosophical intellectualism and meaningless speculations, molded in traditions and repetitions according to mankind's cosmic codes and superstitions and not consistent with Christ. *(Any teaching that leaves you with a sense of lack and imperfection rather than completeness is a distraction from the truth.)*

In the journey of marriage, there are battles that come not only from external forces but from within — battles of beliefs, values, and traditions that seek to define who we are and where we come from.

For us we have had to learn to anchor ourselves from the realm of victory in which Christ has overcome the world. Another one of the biggest challenges is to leave and cleave all our cultural spiritual beliefs, which is all that we have unlearned in order to follow Christ and walk uphill against the deeply-rooted customs of our Xhosa and Tswana heritage.

This was a huge dichotomy because when we observed from the earthly realm without Holy Spirit activating our spiritual gates to discern ourselves in our New Creation position together with Christ, it would be impossible to transcend our cultures. It would be negligence on our part and the Marriage Covenant to deny God's redemption power and identity in Christ. Our walk of Faith, the encounters signs & wonders we've encountered on an individual and corporate level have to count for something.

The subconscious voices and noise streaming through our cultural veins affect our conscious reality. We are not the only beings inhabiting the earth realm, the invisible world exists within and around us. In other words, if one is not born again it is impossible to discern the reality and context of Christ The Most High and the highest supernatural streams of consciousness. It's like having a smartphone disconnected from WiFi, it has the capacity to stream data but is not connected. There are so many things happening around the world but one cannot connect because of no WiFi. So the resistance to cleaving and leaving to Christ as our Husband in a Marriage Covenant is only possible by revelation and wisdom through the person of the Holy Spirit.

Galatians 3:28 TLV

28 There is neither Jew nor Greek, there is neither slave nor free, there is neither male nor female— for you are all one in Messiah *Yeshua*. 29 And if you belong to Messiah, then you are Abraham's seed— heirs according to the promise.

Revelations 5:9 The Mirror

⁹ And they sang a new song saying, "We proclaim your excellent worth! You are the only one in the universe entitled to open the scroll and break its seals, since you were slaughtered in sacrifice and in your blood redeemed mankind's authentic identity in God. You rescued them from everything that could possibly define society before and brought them out of the confines of their dwarfed mindsets. This includes the entire spectrum of people-groupings: our tribal identities, our language-specific dialect preferences, our political and religious associations, as well as every form of racial identity!

The scriptures above are also to be viewed from a revelatory perspective, with the help of the spirit of understanding through Holy Spirit we can understand the nature of our union in Faith.

To be faithful is impossible without God's Grace, our walk of Faith in Christ is a result of His Grace being extended to us of which it is multi-faceted and is a choice of free will we make to receive it in order that our matrimony yields the fruits of Love through the channel of spirit of my spirit, bone of my bones and flesh of my flesh with the last Adam Yeshua Hamashiach.

Every event we experience in the earthly context is always interwoven and rooted from a heavenly context. All events on earth are taking place under heaven's careful observation and God has a great cloud of witnesses cheering us on to walk by Faith.

Hebrews 12:1 The Mirror

¹ So now the stage is set for us: all these faith-heroes cheer us on, as it were, like a great multitude of spectators in the amphitheater. This is our moment. As with an athlete who is determined to win, it would be silly to carry any baggage of the old law-system that would weigh one down. Make sure you do not get your feet clogged up with sin-consciousness.

Become absolutely streamlined in faith. Run the race of your spiritual life with total persuasion.

Our spiritual Identity is therefore the key we need to walk in total freedom from the limitations within our people groups, race and iniquity rooted all the way to the first Adam, in which the record of brother killing brother for revenge happened through Cain and Abel. There is no tribe that has never murdered another person under the sun, all bloodlines have fallen short of the Glory of God. All the records of wrongs have been recorded and are in the books of remembrance which the Accuser uses to get legal rights to attack mankind.

Believe it or not, there is a legal system in Heaven, and until we read this in the bible, and were also mentored through the encounter of deliverance from iniquity in our bloodlines. We got to understand how God was revealed as a Merciful and Gracious Judge. The book of Job begins with Job being described as a rich man who was pleasing before the eyes of God but had children who were always living oblivious to the righteous ways of Job in feastings and pleasures.

Job even had to come before God on their behalf to intercede for them through burnt offerings on his altar with the hope to get them to live in the hedge of God's protection. Satan, "the accuser" had a different plan and wanted their lives because only Job lived within the protection and not his children. Satan was given legal rights to take their lives which is a sad story but a reality of the spiritual realm and the heavenly legal system.

Job 1:4 – 12 AMPC

4 His sons used to go and feast in the house of each on his day (birthday) in turn, and they invited their three sisters to eat and drink with them. 5 And when the days of their feasting were over, Job sent for them to purify and hallow them, and rose up early in the morning and offered burnt offerings according to the number of them all. For Job said, It may be that my sons have sinned and cursed or disowned God in

their hearts. Thus did Job at all [such] times. ⁶ Now there was a day when the sons (the angels) of God came to present themselves before the Lord, and Satan (the adversary and accuser) also came among them. ⁷ And the Lord said to Satan, From where did you come? Then Satan answered the Lord, From going to and fro on the earth and from walking up and down on it. ⁸ And the Lord said to Satan, Have you considered My servant Job, that there is none like him on the earth, a blameless and upright man, one who [reverently] fears God and abstains from and shuns evil [because it is wrong]? ⁹ Then Satan answered the Lord, Does Job [reverently] fear God for nothing? ¹⁰ Have You not put a hedge about him and his house and all that he has, on every side? You have conferred prosperity and happiness upon him in the work of his hands, and his possessions have increased in the land. ¹¹ But put forth Your hand now and touch all that he has, and he will curse You to Your face. ¹² And the Lord said to Satan (the adversary and the accuser), Behold, all that he has is in your power, only upon the man himself put not forth your hand. So Satan went forth from the presence of the Lord.

And we also read that satan had the legal authority beyond the hedge of protection around Job to take the lives of Job's children by manifesting as a whirlwind and took the lives of the children of Job in order to destroy Job's life but God said not to touch Job.

Job 1:18 AMPC

¹⁸While he was yet speaking, there came also another and said, Your sons and your daughters were eating and drinking wine in their eldest brother's house, ¹⁹ And behold, there came a great [whirlwind] from the desert, and smote the four corners of the house, and it fell upon the young people and they are dead, and I alone have escaped to tell you.

Abraham had been told by God in the book of Genesis 12 to leave and cleave to his parents in order for God to bless him fully and multiply his household, although his wife Sarai, was barren. But he did not leave immediately, he stayed with his father, Terah and worshiped other Gods to the detriment of him having to wait even longer to see this come to fruition.

It was only when he left and was obedient to leave that he would enter into his full purpose designed by god for him. Kingdom Biblical principles we strive to uphold will always cost you something, a walk of faith requires us to unlearn and learn in order for God to upgrade and catapult us and our bloodlines into higher dimensions. The conflict between cultural traditions and our faith has not only tested our marriage but also our resolve to walk in alignment with Christ.

Genesis 12: 1 – 2 AMPC

12 Now [in Haran] the Lord said to Abram, Go for yourself [for your own advantage] away from your country, from your relatives and your father's house, to the land that I will show you. 2 And I will make of you a great nation, and I will bless you [with abundant increase of favors] and make your name famous *and* distinguished, and you will be a blessing [dispensing good to others].

Joshua 24: 2 – 3 AMPC

2 Joshua said to all the people, Thus says the Lord, the God of Israel, Your fathers dwelt in olden times beyond the Euphrates River, including Terah the father of Abraham and Nahor, and they served other gods. 3 And I took your father Abraham from beyond the Euphrates River and led him through all the land of Canaan and multiplied his offspring. I gave him Isaac,

[1] And the high priest asked [Stephen], Are these charges true? [2] And he answered, Brethren and fathers, listen to me! The God of glory appeared to our forefather Abraham when he was still in Mesopotamia, before he [went to] live in Haran, [3] And He said to him, Leave your own country and your relatives and come into the land (region) that I will point out to you. [4] So then he went forth from the land of the Chaldeans and settled in Haran. And from there, after his father died, [God] transferred him to this country in which you are now dwelling.

From the beginning, we understood that blending our lives would require a delicate balance of honoring our cultural backgrounds while building a life based on our shared Kingdom faith in Christ Yeshua Hamashiach, The King of kings. However, as we navigated this complex terrain, we quickly realized that the road ahead would be far from smooth.

Both the Xhosa and Tswana cultures are rich in tradition, with rituals and customs passed down through generations. These traditions serve as a link to the past, a way of preserving the identity and values of the community. Yet, as we are biologically Tswana and Xhosa, the born again spiritual birth could not be overlooked, nor ignored when we began to delve deeper into our spiritual journey. We began to question the relevance and alignment of some of these traditions with our faith in Christ.

One of the most challenging aspects of this journey was the pressure from some of our family members to adhere to certain traditional rituals that conflicted with our Christian beliefs. Among these were practices involving the consulting of spiritual mediums, the burning of incense to invoke the presence of ancestors, and other rituals intended to honor the spirits of the deceased. Whilst these practices held deep significance for our families, Holy Spirit revealed to us the ramifications they will have and the impact on our bloodlines for future generations. We felt a growing conviction that our true allegiance lay with Christ alone. We have friends who have testimonies which gave us insight of growing up with parents that were traditional healers and sangomas who were expected to inherit the powers and mantles from their parents when they died.

One of them says it was a spiritual warfare because he had become born again and had wanted nothing to do with their old bloodline tribal practices. Yet his elders would do all they could in their power to manipulate and even make him suffer long, taking it to the extent that he would be cursed to suffer financially. For a season, he lived on the streets as a homeless person.

He outlived his father's wishes, who had passed on. His last parting words were to his amazement at the strength of the God, to help him resist spiritually the ancestral powers and mantle to escape the grip of an ancestral bloodline contract to fall on him. Now his mother today is a changed woman who is devoted to Yeshua Hamashiach and has encountered Christ for herself, to the devotion of working in prison ministry to share God's love with all the downcast and forgotten. It sounds all good at the end, but he paid a price.

Psalm 119: 99 AMPC

99 I have better understanding *and* deeper insight than all my teachers, because Your testimonies are my meditation.

It is from these testimonies that we gained understanding and Holy Spirit gave us more insight in the discerning of spirits. He revealed that whenever someone in the bloodline, in this case, a family member, goes and seeks a medium to look into the future progress of their children in the bloodline, they open up an illegal door into their children's lives, aware or unaware. This exposes them to the demonic oppression of familiar and monitoring spirits, etc., which can cause strife in their marriage relationship. It is even more hectic when it is a situation where we do not share the same beliefs.

I (Legae) was being called by my mother to tell me that my wife was a witch, and this was shown to her in her dreams and confirmed by her medium. It is the fate of many young born again believers who have fallen by the way side in captivity because the automatic inclination for a son to their mother would be to believe the cultural saying that "there is no love more deeper than a mother's love for her son", but I have found that actually there is no better love than Yeshua Hamashiach's Love my creator who loved me before the foundations of the earth, died for my sins and took all iniquity upon himself so I could live free, such that by the time he sends me to earth to be born into my mother's womb I would transition timeously to leave and cleave untethering from the traditions that bind me to reach the highest potential which is to receive eternal life. God's plans indeed are never to harm me. Imagine choosing to divorce my wife and leave my children fatherless because of rumors told to my mother by spiritual mediums.

I would be told by my own biological mother that I was bewitched, even to be married by a Xhosa woman who is a witch. We already knew that when these mediums are being consulted, and they want to intrude in the affairs of Born Again Faithful believers who are married, they will sow division and conflict by creating problems between their client and the client's family. We saw many of these case studies through the great ministry of Mama and Pastor Irene Tshifiwa, who used to run a marathon of stadium ministry evangelical events across the continent, delivering people from all sorts of witchcraft and satanic snares. Whenever a witch-doctor was being delivered we understood the language was that Born Again believers were also believed to be practicing witchcraft from their side of the world of darkness. So we were not shocked, but just not expecting it to also happen to us.

If I had not read in the bible that Moses was criticized by Mariam and Aaron for having married the daughter of another tribe from Cush and given them leprosy for that, I would have been devastated.

Numbers 12:1 AMPC

12 Then Miriam and Aaron spoke against Moses on

account of the Cushite woman he married, because he had married a Cushite woman.

Thank God I had my full armor and became even meek to immunity from the onslaught. If many ancient years ago, "The Moses" was also ill-treated by his own in-laws, then with God on our side, we would live to see victory like them by God's Grace and have peace amongst our family. I would have fallen for the old cultural saying "blood is thicker than water", but I tell you the blood of Yeshua Hamashiach speaks better things than all the fallen tribes of this world, to the redeeming of every nation tongue and tribe, grafting me into his family as a royal priest to minister unto the Most High as in the book of Revelation.

Revelation 5:9-10 AMPC

[9] And [now] they sing a new song, saying, You are worthy to take the scroll and to break the seals that are on it, for You were slain (sacrificed), and with Your blood You purchased men unto God from every tribe and language and people and nation. [10] And You have made them a kingdom (royal race) and priests to our God, and they shall reign [as kings] over the earth!

(Legae) I hope someone appreciates the Power of reading the Bible as an instrument and gateway to enter into the encounters and see that God is the same in the past, present, and will remain constant in the future to deliver his own from the sacred traditions that bind us negatively. I know this may appear controversial, but I am leaving these breadcrumbs for many young married couples to understand that when we choose to get married as Born Again believers in a Marriage Covenant to Christ we are declaring Victory over the war of the laws of sin and death, which is divorce of Adam and Eve from their Creator in the Beginning.

DISCLAIMER: These principles are available to all but unique to only Born Again Believers who commit to a life of Faith in Yeshua Hamashiach's revelation of Covenant Marriage and the Resurrected Christ, The Messiah.

2 Corinthians 10: 4-6 AMPC

⁴ For the weapons of our warfare are not physical [weapons of flesh and blood], but they are mighty before God for the overthrow *and* destruction of strongholds, ⁵ [Inasmuch as we] refute arguments *and* theories *and* reasonings and every proud *and* lofty thing that sets itself up against the [true] knowledge of God; and we lead every thought *and* purpose away captive into the obedience of Christ (the Messiah, the Anointed One), ⁶ Being in readiness to punish every disobedience, when your own submission *and* obedience [as a church] are fully secured *and* complete.

These weapons can only protect us as The Bride of Christ when our own submission and obedience are fully secured and complete. Our protection from external forces coming to divide us can only be exposed when we have submitted ourselves to Unconditional Love in Christ for each other. Those who love us on condition that we will be in their bad books for not choosing our marriage relationship in Christ will be Loved by us Unconditionally by His Grace even when they show us conditional love.

This mystery of Unconditional Love will expose the foundation and boundaries of the type of Love we profess to walk in, it will be the realm in which our Marriage Covenant will be hidden in and the fortress which will be our protection from those who are with us and against us. This is difficult for believers on the fence, either you unlearn and learn new things or be caught by the snares of traditions that bind us. I know a lot of men who "who claimed to be believers in Christ" ended up divorcing their wives who were at the receiving end of traditions that bind us. To cleave and leave is impossible without Faith. If your spiritual eyes and ears are not mature, this is what we term "missed call" and casualties will be incurred for a lack of discernment of spirits. Unconditional Love also helps us to walk in Love despite the disagreements in beliefs and practices our families and relatives practice.

It is easy to be pulled into judgmentalism rather than the righteous Judgement that comes with forgiving and letting God fight your battles through His Heavenly just legal system. Our Unconditional Love has been put to the test and taken to extremes, like we had said before that Long Suffering and Self Control is the fruits of the Spirit.

Matthew 11:12 AMPC

¹² And from the days of John the Baptist until the present time, the kingdom of heaven has endured violent assault, and violent men seize it by force [as a precious prize—a share in the heavenly kingdom is sought with most ardent zeal and intense exertion].

There are so many years of insults and emotional abuse that were hurled at me for staying true and faithful to my Covenant Marriage in Christ that I understood I had to create boundaries to protect my family. God revealed the depth of the bondage my mother had gotten herself into, and as I prayed to God for her deliverance, I was given even more peace, empathy, and insight into the effects it had over my younger siblings. Old unforgiveness, coupled with the past hurts that my biological father's fallout with my mother went through, including the records of old grievances from their failed marriage were being projected over and hemorrhaging through my interactions with them. This is my story, and these events contributed to a poverty mindset which affected us on many levels without us realizing.

I thought we were the only ones going through this, but it has become a tradition that binds our families, and only by His Grace have we overcome. The bigger picture is that we drew a line from the onset that this generational curse of divorce in my family would end with us in our generation.

Ephesians 6: 2 – 3 AMPC

[2] Honor (esteem and value as precious) your father and your mother— this is the first commandment with a promise— [3] That all may be well with you and that you may live long on the earth.

Another snare that the accuser uses against us believers in Christ is to manipulate us by tempting us into dishonoring our parents. If you have read this far, it means if you come to observe that we believe that the written words in the bible are the Word of God in our household and we have aspired to encounter the Word to be real in our lives.

2 Timothy 3: 16 – 17 AMPC

[16] Every Scripture is God-breathed (given by His inspiration) and profitable for instruction, for reproof *and* conviction of sin, for correction of error *and* discipline in obedience, [and] for training in righteousness (in holy living, in conformity to God's will in thought, purpose, and action), [17] So that the man of God may be complete *and* proficient, well fitted *and* thoroughly equipped for every good work.

The accuser knows the eternal ramification of dishonor, he knows that it can bring us out of alignment with Divinity. He understands that divorce is a great weapon and he even knows how it impacts the next generation of children raised in the generational curse. If he can get us to dishonor our parents, then technically we may not live well and live long on earth.

The opposite is also crucial, as parents, we cannot be found as bad stewards and custodians of this sacred ministry of Marriage. We are responsible also to administrate the presence of God's Love and encounters, firstly through our earthly interaction and secondly through the manifestation of a supernatural lifestyle of Heaven's atmosphere in our homes. Failing to do so, we will cause our children to experience a closed heaven over them, and that trauma hinders their encounter with their Creator in the future for a bigger purpose than our own.

Ephesians 6: 4 AMPC

[4] **Fathers, do not irritate *and* provoke your children to anger [do not exasperate them to resentment], but rear them [tenderly] in the training *and* discipline and the counsel *and* admonition of the Lord.**

Matthew 19: 14 AMPC

[14] **But He said, Leave the children alone! Allow the little ones to come to Me, and do not forbid *or* restrain *or* hinder them, for of such [as these] is the kingdom of heaven *composed*.**

Matthew 18: 10 AMPC

[10] **Beware that you do not despise *or* feel scornful toward *or* think little of one of these little ones, for I tell you that in heaven their angels always are in the presence of *and* look upon the face of My Father Who is in heaven.**

Whenever we felt we were put in a compromising and conflicting position by our parents about this revelation, which God brought before us. We sought the Lord's face and came into repentance, asking Him to shed light on this matter. We came to the revelation that Unconditional Love goes deeper than what we think or understand. We came to receive it as a default setting for us to stay in God's Perfect Will for Marriage, and when He revealed to us that in The Trinity, He is our Primordial Father before the Foundation of the Earth, and that all things that are good and righteous can only be associated with Him as source. We have the power of free will to receive his transmission of Unconditional Love or we can believe the lie that we manifest as parents to our beloved children or have experienced in our upbringing. No parent wants to be caught in the vicious cycle of being the prey after crying innocently as the victim.

We cannot repeat the cycle, and we refuse to be caught as the victims. Hence, in the book of Galatians and James, we get a picture of an encounter by Paul and James who experience God as our Heavenly Father and also Jerusalem as the Mother of the Living. Thus, meaning "Jerusalem" being "The City of Shalom/Peace" on Earth is a concept taken from the precept from the Heavenly Jerusalem - The Holy City of Zion. May I present this reality that if you Honor (esteem and value as precious) your Heavenly Father and your Heavenly Mother, this is the first commandment with a promise— [3] That all may be well with you and that you may live long on the earth.

When we got married, we not only began a family, we were plugged into a system of fellowship with families in the Kingdom of God where cross-generational families were living in harmony. We were learning under the mentorship of our spiritual mothers and fathers how to raise our kids under the family banner of Christ. We were also taking notes, absorbing all the lessons we missed from living in single-headed households and how to be a loving family throughout the highs and lows of life. We learnt how to honour and receive honour from God through our spiritual family and became a wholesome family unit that will not produce cancerous cells to the bigger body of society.

The bible in the book of Ezekiel 28 shows us through the prophet of God Ezekiel, that the accuser "satan" used to work as a cherubim of God before he fell from the presence of God.

Ezekiel 28: 13 -15 AMPC

[13] You were in Eden, the garden of God; every precious stone was your covering, the carnelian, topaz, jasper, chrysolite, beryl, onyx, sapphire, carbuncle, and emerald; and your settings and your sockets *and* engravings were wrought in gold. On the day that you were created they were prepared. [14] You were the anointed cherub that covers with overshadowing [wings], and I set you so. You were

upon the holy mountain of God; you walked up and down in the midst of the stones of fire [like the paved work of gleaming sapphire stone upon which the God of Israel walked on Mount Sinai]. [15] You were blameless in your ways from the day you were created until iniquity *and* guilt were found in you.

It is absolutely naive to think the devil is a fool and he doesn't know the working of heaven and the Word of God in order to pervert it and create counterattacks. He is an ancient fallen being who has created counterfeit heavens and systemic poverty in such a cunning way that humanity has blamed God for all the problems we see. "Why do bad things happen to good people?" has become the auto tune for countless questions asked without finding answers.

It is written there by prophet Ezekiel that iniquity was found in satan and when satan was given the rights to the earthly kingdom by Adam, iniquity entered into the bloodline and DNA of man. The accuser has a legal right to tempt you to obey him through free will, and if you walk in the dark, you will believe every system of lying, stealing and destruction he will tempt you with to give up on a Covenant Marriage with Yeshua Hamashiach.

We have learned to walk in the Peace of God because the plan of the enemy for us to dishonor our parents on Earth would legally prevail if we refuse to walk in Unconditional Love to the detriment of living long in Eternal Life. Complaining and walking in unforgiveness and anger was distorting God's open heaven over us, and it affected god's blessing over our lives for a season. Blaming our biological parents could no longer hold water, for the Truth is meant to set us free from all the worry, all it requires us is to seek first The King, His Righteousness and His Kingdom, and all the benefits will be automatically added to us through citizenship. Heaven on Earth is real. God's Love is amongst us! The real uphill battle is changing our mindset, heart-set, and gut-set…food for our spirit souls and body must totally change. What we grew up believing is healthy needs to change holistically for us to have a long life.

Our favourite meals that we grew up on, which pose health hazards, cannot suffice going forward in our generation. If there is a history of people dying of diabetes in the family, should we continue to buy and eat food that aggravates diabetes in our grocery? Do we believe all the advertising, even to the destruction of our health? Do we keep those foods in our households because it was our parents' favourite when they visited us? Or do we introduce and replace those old traditions that bind us with better and healthy traditions that bring liberty?

It will be an uphill battle to change tradition, but for us, it has been choosing life instead of death. It takes one generation to choose to be a blessing and uproot a generational curse from another generation.

During the Sermon on the Mount, Yeshua Hamashiach speaks about the Beatitudes.

Matthew 5:5 AMPC

5 "Blessed are the meek, for they shall inherit the earth".

Holy Spirit revealed to us that the opposite of meek is anger. It is the iniquity in satan that entered through Adam and Eve, giving birth to the bloodline of human species that ate from the tree of good and evil. We observe how sin blossomed throughout the earth as Cain's anger and jealousy grew to the extent of him killing his own brother and causing the earth to drink blood.

In the letters of the book of Galatians, Apostle Paul writes about how important the 9 fruits of the spirit Love, Peace, Joy, Humility, Meekness, Gentleness, Long Suffering, Patience, and Self-Control are. He makes emphasis on another one of his famous letters in the book of 1 Corinthians, chapter 12, the importance of the gifts of the Spirit to enable believers to do the work of God.

He reveals how all these beautiful and wonderful gifts are given by Holy Spirit and to be used for the work of ministry in our daily lives within the fivefold ministry as believers. In the next chapter of 1 Corinthians 13, he then expands to say these gifts of the spirit can be abused if the person operating in them is not rooted in the fruit of the spirit, Love. We have learnt that it is important in our marriage to stay rooted in Christ when we flow in the gifts of the Holy Spirit. When we posture our hearts in the Unconditional Love of God, there becomes a distinction between flowing in the Holy Spirit and familiar spirits. Without Love we can be deceived and operate from a realm of divination or mediums.

Operating in the 9 gifts of the spirit as described in 1 Corinthians 12 without being anchored in the 9 fruits of the Spirit is a formula for disaster. We love our mother, and only by Grace we have overcome the negativity. If we had not understood that we were not fighting flesh and blood, we would have been long lost in the lying, stealing and destructive plans of the enemy of marriage long time ago. God gave us a revelation that choosing divorce is choosing pride over Humility.

In Luke Chapter 4, when Yeshua Hamashiach was fasting in the wilderness for forty days and nights, we observe that Yeshua, embodying the spirit of Humility, was face to face with satan pride himself. The thing they both have in common is they both have a history with YHWH. Satan, the king of pride, and Yeshua Hamashiach The King of Humility, a Servant and Son of God.

Job 41:34 KJV

[34] He beholdeth all high things: he is a king over all the children of pride.

Divorce in marriage relationship is Pride and Leviathan leads that rebellion attacking the image of our Covenant Marriage. It requires submitting to each other and can only be possible through God's Grace and Humility. The iniquity in our bloodlines has cast an eternal shadow of pride deep in our DNA since the fall of Adam and Eve. That is why we are all born into sin because of the nature of the impurities passed down through our tribal bloodlines including DNA records of sin.

Look at the nations that kill babies before they are born through legal frameworks for a profit. Is it not written in the Book of Exodus that pharaoh wanted to kill Hebrew boys? In the book of Matthew that Yeshua was sought after by Herod to kill him and all the children of the same age in the region? And in the Book of Revelation that there was a dragon who seeks to eat children before they were born?

Exodus 1: 15 - 17 TLV

15 Moreover the king of Egypt spoke to the Hebrew midwives, one of whom was named Shiphrah and the other Puah, 16 and said, "When you help the Hebrew women during childbirth, look at the sex. If it's a son, then kill him, but if it's a daughter, she may live." 17 Yet the midwives feared God, so they did not do as the king of Egypt commanded them, but let the boys live.

Matthew 2:13 TLV

13 Now when they had gone, behold, an angel of ADONAI appears to Joseph in a dream, saying, "Get up! Take the Child and His mother and flee to Egypt. Stay there until I tell you, for Herod is about to search for the Child, to kill Him."

Revelations 12: 3 - 4 The Mirror

3 Then another sign showed up in the sky - a monster sized red Dragon with seven heads and ten horns. 4 And with his tail he dragged a third of the stars and flung them upon the earth. The heads were wrapped in royal diadems. He then positioned himself in front of the woman and threatened to devour the child as soon as it was born.

The tension reached its peak when family members began to suggest that the struggles and storms we were facing — such as financial setbacks, health challenges, and marital tensions — were the result of our neglect of ancestral worship. The insinuation that our troubles were due to our failure to honor our ancestors weighed heavily on us, creating a rift that threatened to tear apart the peace and harmony of our marriage.

We were not alone in our struggle. We found solace and strength in the words of Colossians 2:8, which warned us to be wary of being led astray by the traditions of men and the rudiments of the world. This scripture became a guiding light, reminding us that our ultimate loyalty is to Christ, not to the customs of our forefathers.

Yet, the battle was far from over. In addition to the cultural challenges, we faced another formidable opponent: the rapidly changing landscape of the modern world. The rise of technologies like Artificial Intelligence, Blockchain, Virtual Reality, and the Fourth Industrial Revolution (4IR) posed new challenges for the church, which seemed to be lagging behind in adapting to these advancements. As professionals in the ICT Media sector, we've been acutely aware of the church's struggle to remain relevant in an increasingly digital and interconnected world.

Our unique perspective — a Biblical, media-centric worldview — (how the Word of God has transitioned from print publishing to virtual reality) led us to question some of the ancient practices and worldly rituals rooted in the tree of knowledge of good and evil that the church community continued to uphold. As we analyzed the church's approach to engaging with the real world, we found ourselves increasingly disillusioned with what we saw as lukewarm traditions that no longer served our intended purpose.

This shift in perspective brought about a wave of innovation and a deep desire to see the church evolve to meet the needs of the present and future. But our efforts to spark change were often met with resistance. It was as if, by questioning the status quo, we were stirring a hornet's nest. The backlash from both within and outside the church was intense, testing our resolve and our commitment to our mission.

In the marketplace, I (Legae) faced significant temptations

to compromise my values. On more than one occasion, I was propositioned to engage in unethical practices, including committing adultery, in exchange for lucrative business deals. These moments of temptation were profound tests of our faith and the strength of my union with Tammy. Only by the Grace of God and the revelation of oneness in Christ was Legae able to withstand these temptations, discerning that his spiritual heritage and birthright were far more valuable than any material gain.

The pain of seeing others seemingly prosper by compromising our values was difficult to bear. We watched as those who chose to pursue wealth at the expense of their integrity often met tragic ends — marriages crumbled, fraudulent activities were exposed, and some even lost their lives. It was a stark reminder of the words of Mark 8:36: "For what shall it profit a man, if he shall gain the whole world, and lose his own soul?"

The struggles we faced were not just about cultural traditions or the pressures of modernity. They were about the deeper question of what truly binds us — what gives our lives meaning and purpose. Is it the rituals and customs handed down through generations, or is it the eternal truths found in Christ Yeshua? Through our journey, we discovered that while traditions have our place, we must always be evaluated in Light of God's Word. It is Christ who binds us together, who gives us our true identity, and who leads us through the storms of life. This revelation allowed us to stand firm in our faith, even when it meant going against the expectations of our families and the pressures of society.

Sacred rituals to ponder on for Couples to Weather Storms of Tradition and Belief

1. Engage in Regular Spiritual Reflection:

    - Set aside time to reflect on the traditions and beliefs that you hold. Discuss how we align with your faith in Christ. This practice helps ensure that your values and practices are consistent with your spiritual convictions.

2. Prayer and Fasting:

- When faced with challenging decisions, especially those involving cultural or spiritual conflicts, consider prayer and fasting as a way to seek God's guidance. This can bring clarity and peace in the midst of difficult choices.

3. Open Dialogue with Family:

- Have honest and respectful conversations with family members about your beliefs and the choices you make. While these conversations may be difficult, they are essential for maintaining relationships whilst staying true to your faith.

4. Seek Wise Counsel:

- Surround yourselves with mentors or spiritual leaders who can offer guidance and wisdom, especially when navigating complex cultural or spiritual issues. Their experience and insight can be invaluable.

5. Create New Traditions:

- Consider creating new traditions that reflect your shared faith and values. These can serve as a bridge between your cultural heritage and your spiritual beliefs, honoring both without compromising your convictions.

6. Study Scripture Together:

- Delve into the Bible together to gain a deeper understanding of how to apply God's word to your life and decisions. Scripture is the ultimate authority, and studying it together can strengthen your bond and provide direction.

7. Stay Informed and Adapt:

- In a rapidly changing world, it's important to stay informed about new developments, especially in areas like technology and culture. Discuss how these changes affect your faith and your roles in the world, and be willing to adapt while staying grounded in biblical principles.

8. Support Each Other in Temptation:

- Temptations will come, but facing them together can make all the difference. Be each other's accountability partners, offering support, encouragement, and prayer to resist compromises that go against your values.

9. Celebrate Your Victories:

- When you overcome a storm or successfully navigate a challenging situation, take time to celebrate. Acknowledge God's hand in your journey and give thanks together for the strength and wisdom He provides.

As we continued to walk this path, we realized that the rituals that truly liberate us are not those rooted in cultural traditions, but those found in our Covenant Relationship with Yeshua The Christ. The rituals of prayer, worship, and communion with God are some of what give our lives meaning and strength. As we embraced this truth, we found The Peace that surpassed all understanding, a peace that allowed us to weather any storm that came our way.

In the end, it is not the traditions of men that will save us, but the unchanging truth of God's Word. It is in this truth that we found the courage to stand firm, to honor our heritage in a way that glorified God, and to forge a path that was uniquely our own, guided by the Light of Christ.

CHAPTER 6

UNBREAKABLE THREADS AND LOVE ACROSS TIME AND DISTANCE

THE ANCIENT PATH OF LOVE

Ecclesiastes 4:12

A cord of three strands is not quickly broken.

The precept of walking in the spirit by Faith as outlined in the scriptures, is a journey both mysterious and profound. It is a path that demands more than just the mind's understanding—it requires the soul's surrender, the heart's alignment, and the spirit's constant communion with the Holy Divine. For us, this journey has not merely been theoretical; it became the bedrock of our relationship, especially in the trying season when physical distance threatened to strain our bond. We had a season when we lived for almost one year apart from each other because Tammy had to live 1000km for work.

Jeremiah 6:16 NIV

This is what the LORD says: 'Stand at the crossroads and look; ask for the ancient paths, ask where the good way is, and walk in it, and you will find rest for your souls.'

The ancient path, as Prophet Jeremiah speaks of, is literal and abstract in its essence. It calls for a deeper understanding, one that goes beyond the visible and tangible. Walking in love, as instructed by the person of The Holy Spirit, is an act of faith—a decision to trust in someone greater than oneself, to believe in the power of the unseen. In our context, this meant trusting in the strength of our Love, even when we were miles apart, trusting that the same Spirit who had united us in the beginning would keep us strong through the storms of life.

Romans 8:35-37 NIV

Who shall separate us from the love of Christ? Shall trouble or hardship or persecution or famine or nakedness or danger or sword? ... No, in all these things we are more than conquerors through him who loved us.

UNBREAKABLE THREADS

Ecclesiastes 4 NKJV

[12] And though a man might prevail against him who is alone, two will withstand him. A threefold cord is not quickly broken.

The image of a cord of three strands written by King Solomon in Ecclesiastes 4:12 beautifully captures the essence of a love that is fortified by faith. When two are joined together, we can withstand much. But when the third strand—representing the Spirit of God—is intertwined with us, our bond becomes unbreakable. This was the reality for us and many who have walked through these rites of passage in the mystical oneness. Our love, tested by distance and time, grew stronger, not weaker.

Tammy's work took her 1000 kilometers away from home, and for close to a year, she could only visit us once a month. The physical separation was painful for me (Legae), who was naturally used to physical touch and quality time as my Love language, especially for our youngest son, Olebogeng, who missed his mother's cooking.

The longing to be together was intense, but it was this very longing that deepened our love. The bond between us was like a chemical compound, where atoms, once bonded, create a substance stronger than the sum of its parts. Our love was not merely a feeling; it was a force, a living testament to the power of unity in Christ.

During this time, we clung to the promises found in Ecclesiastes 4:9-12. We understood that two are indeed better than one, for we can support and strengthen each other. Even though we were apart, we worked together, supporting one another through regular prayer, calling each other on a daily basis, having fellowship with other prayer groups consistently, and serving on ministries in the body of Christ around the cities of our dwelling, and the shared hope of being reunited would always be with a fresh anticipation. This physical separation, rather than weakening our marriage, became a crucible in which our love was purified and strengthened.

A SEASON OF GROWTH

The experience was not easy, especially for our children. Olebogeng, our youngest, had to adapt to homeschooling in a new environment, away from his father and older brother, Rethabile. Meanwhile, I (Legae) stayed behind in Pretoria, living in an international student accommodation provided by a friend from church, and offered a time to minister Christ's Love to international and local students. Although it was a challenging time, it was also a period of growth and spiritual enrichment for the entire family.

For me (Legae), this season became a time of deep spiritual encounters. The longing to be with Tammy mirrored the revelation of the longing Christ has for His Bride, the Church. Each trip to see Tammy became a sacred journey, filled with anticipation and love. It was as if I could feel, in some small way, the heart of God, who longs to be reunited with His people in the final days. This spiritual insight brought a renewed depth to my faith and understanding of His Divine Love.

LOVE KNOWS NO DISTANCE

Our experience is a powerful reminder that love knows no distance. When a bond is formed in the Spirit, it transcends physical separation. The love that is rooted in Christ cannot be easily broken by the trials of this world. It is this love that sustained us through our season of separation, and it is this same love that continues to bind us together today.

Our story is a testament to the power of a three-stranded cord. The support of family and friends, the prayers of our church community, and the strength of our faith all contributed to our resilience. It is a story of hope for any couple facing similar challenges—a reminder that with God at the center, no distance is too great, and no trial too difficult to overcome. When I met young single men, and they asked me how I (Legae) do it? How do I stay committed to my wife so much and not get distracted by the stereotypical disruptive behavior?

My response was always, "I am in a Covenant Marriage with God, I am a father and mentor to many, I enjoy my life in Christ, and because I am whole and content, I do not need anything outside of Christ to satisfy me. God is more than enough! El Shaddai!"

In this season, I made new friends with a younger generation of believers and visited their youth ministries in Pretoria, Hatfield. I began to record music, and my passion to intercede with tertiary youth from all walks of life was ignited.

I was led by Holy Spirit to join an international movement of Global Sons, which connected me with a network of ministries across 6 continents, training up spiritual sons to learn how to walk in God's Identity and spiritual maturity in Christ.

The world became too small, and weeks went by and by as we shared our growth and business opportunities we found that God strengthened our bond together with Him, both together and individually for this season before he got us to re-unite again.

KEEPING THE FIRE BURNING:

Practical Tips for Long-Distance Relationships. For couples who find themselves in similar situations, there are several practical ways to keep the fire burning:

1. Daily Communication: Make time for daily calls or video chats. Even a few minutes of connection can make a big difference.

2. Prayer and Devotions Together: Praying together, even over the phone, strengthens the spiritual bond. Consider reading the same devotional or scripture passage and discussing it.

3. Plan Visits and Countdowns: Whenever possible, plan visits and create a countdown. Knowing when you'll see each other next gives you something to look forward to.

4. Surprise Letters or Gifts: Send letters, small gifts, or care packages. These surprises can make the distance feel less daunting. God can inspire us to be creative when we ask with purpose and intent.

5. Share Your Day: Share details about your day, no matter how mundane. This helps maintain a sense of normalcy and closeness.

6. Lean on Community: It's been a blessing and a privilege to be able to ask for help from our spiritual community—family, friends, and church. Their support has always been invaluable.

7. Meditate on God's Promises: Reflect on scriptures that emphasize unity, love, and strength in Christ. Let these be your anchor in difficult times.

CONCLUSION

Our story is one of perseverance, faith, and an unbreakable bond. We have been walking the ancient path of love, a path that is mysterious yet filled with the assurance of God's Presence. We have discovered that love, when intertwined with the Spirit, is a powerful force that can withstand any storm. Our journey, though marked by challenges, is a beautiful testament to the enduring power of love and faith.

CHAPTER 7

COUPLES OF THE BIBLE

BUTTERFLICATION

In 2015, at the ACM (Association for Christian Media), a gentleman by the name Patrick Kuwana gave a devotion about the journey from being a believer to being a Bride. It was profound and indelible leaving a deep impression on my perception of what it really meant to be married for us. When he spoke, we discerned the spirit of wisdom over that message and saw a vision of a parallel picture of nature and creation, the metamorphosis of the believer to a bride as an egg to a butterfly. Now, when recalling the message with maturity many years later in 2025, let us journey together through the Butterflication phases as God has revealed afresh. Let us also behold and appreciate the manifold dynamic levels of the multiverse

(Thy will be done, as it is in heaven also on earth) mandates that married and corporate ministries in the body of Christ are available. We hope that this inspires us all to keep growing from glory to glory and refuse to plateau, settling for stale bread when the Mercies and the Bread of Life is to be received daily.

DOOR ONE: BEING BORN AGAIN

John 3: 3 The Message

³ Jesus said, "You're absolutely right. Take it from me: Unless a person is born from above, it's not possible to see what I'm pointing to—to God's kingdom."

The womb of our earthly mothers is a blessing. It is the divine doorway to which our spirits are knit around flesh to legally live in the earthly realm. Without the human body, the soul and spirit have no anchor or business existing on Earth. In our context as married couples, it is a blessing to have been married to Christ and one another as a couple. Our church administered our spiritual birth and encounter for us to be reconciled with our Father in Heaven and to be in Covenant Marriage with Christ Yeshua. Thus, to be equally yoked, to believe in the same things and the same God, not only has it made navigating life's mountains and valleys together much sweeter, but it has also made us closer to God. As much as we have roles and responsibilities to walk in the Light as New Creations in Christ, it is beautiful to see that the people we were when we met are totally different from the people we are now. We have developed spiritual eyes for each other and are forever drinking from each others well through Christ who makes it all well. Whenever we sense there is a deviation from our ID's in Christ about who we are, we hold each other accountable and get out of our way to maintain oneness at all cost.

Unlearning the old life of the kingdom of darkness is a daily carrying of our cross and as Christ is The Head of our head (Legae) and the Body (Tammy) We fit into the Body of Christ with our unique ID's perfectly as one in Christ. The natural outflow as evangelists to constantly lead souls to reconciliation with Our Father's Love, supernaturally takes center stage as a lifestyle of administering the revelation of Unconditional Love and Oneness in Christ our Lord. Yeshua Hamashiach is The Multi-Dimensional Doorways (The Way, The Truth & The Life) of Marriage into manifold wisdoms of The Bridegroom Mysterion.

DOOR TWO: BEING A DISCIPLE

Matthew 28: 18 – 20 AMPC

[18] Jesus approached and, breaking the silence, said to them, All authority (all power of rule) in heaven and on earth has been given to Me. [19] Go then and make disciples of all the nations, baptizing them into the name of the Father and of the Son and of the Holy Spirit, [20] Teaching them to observe everything that I have commanded you,

When our sons were old enough and could comprehend the reality of Christ, we did not waste time to baptize them at home. It is a blessing to be led by Holy Spirit as a family to the sensitivity of discerning the rapid changes that this generation faces. Immediately when we picked up that their adolescent stage came with its overwhelming desire to explore the world, we were led to water baptism at home.

Pst. Simphiwe Kondlo would always caution us to watch, that we do not go out teaching the Gospel to the public and neglect to minister first in our own households. This pattern was important to observe as we were patient to communicate our stance to everyone around our family circles, that we are disciples of Christ, and 19 years later, in 2025 are still being perfected in the discipline of Christ's Covenant Unconditional Love.

This has helped much because our children always discern who to be friends with at school, and when we follow up their friends' family backgrounds, to our amazement, it is families from households who are aligned with our beliefs in God. Family and friends will then learn by how we conduct ourselves that we are set apart for God. We have had many instances where even elders from both sides of our family acknowledge our straight and narrow path of following Christ as a pattern to follow. Sharing our testimony is at the tip of our tongue, and signs, miracles, and wonders have been witnessed over the years. From healing prayers, to resurrecting marriages in the state of dry bones, to supernatural provisions etc. As we journey together, our inner circle of friends and family in the Lord will be made known, and the diverse testimonies from walking with Christ will be made known to the public.

DOOR THREE: BEING A SERVANT

Joshua 24: 14 – 16 AMPC

14 Now therefore, [reverently] fear the Lord and serve Him in sincerity and in truth; put away the gods which your fathers served on the other side of the [Euphrates] River and in Egypt, and serve the Lord. 15 And if it seems evil to you to serve the Lord, choose for yourselves this day whom you will serve, whether the gods which your fathers served on the other side of the River, or the gods of the Amorites, in whose land you dwell; but as for me and my house, we will serve the Lord. 16 The people answered, Far be it from us to forsake the Lord to serve other gods;

The first time we heard a bold statement of servanthood in the Bible was when Joshua had just taken over the leadership position from Moses after walking 40 years in the desert. Remember Joshua and Caleb were about to be stoned for daring to believe that serving the God who just helped them cross over the Red Sea, which swallowed Pharaoh's army whole, would again give them victory against the giants in the promised land. They were on the verge of being stoned to death until Moses intervened.

When God responded to Moses' inquiry he said to Moses, to remember to allow Joshua and Caleb to be the first people in line to choose the best parts of the Promised land because they believed Him as a Powerful and Faithful God. The punishment for the rest of the unbelieving nation was 1 year for every day of the 40 days the 10 spies took to get to the promised land. Israel had no faith to trust and serve God, even after seeing the size of the grapes; they believed the lie that the giants were bigger than their God's Government and Power, and thus, their punishment was forty years in the desert for trying to kill Joshua and Caleb for having been there and believed in God.

Now, because of the lack of faith to serve God by the rest of the nation, Joshua and Caleb suffered persecution and had to walk with a generation of disobedient, unfaithful servants of Israel. When they all passed on, the next generation would enter the promised land. Upon entering, he said to all of Israel that they should choose which God they would follow, the Gods of Egypt, which their parents followed, or the Gods of the Amorites, which they were about to conquer. He announced that He and His family would not repeat the same mistake and anyone in the way of them and their God will have to face the same wrath indirectly. They chose to serve God and had a supernatural backing of the army of God's angels every step of the way until Joshua passed on.

Unlearning to fear man and learning to fear God is the process of being a servant. Seeing a pillar of fire by night and a cloud by day was healthy for Joshua's younger generation to discern the power of God daily. As we serve God, we learn to walk in the supernatural, we learn how to exercise authority with the angelic help by His Grace and access the abundance of Heaven's Daily bread as it is in Heaven.

Mark 10: 43 – 45 AMPC

43 But this is not to be so among you; instead, whoever desires to be great among you must be your servant, 44 And whoever wishes to be most important and first in rank among you must be slave of all. 45 For even the Son of Man came not to have service rendered to Him, but to serve, and to give His life as a ransom for (instead of) many.

This model of Yeshua as a King being a servant was very foreign to me, because the world we live in and its kings have primarily focused on what they can get from the masses, but this Eternal Kingdom Principle requires that to be kings and queens, we must be the servants of all with Unconditional Love. It means nothing in the worldly and secular sense until we have to measure the number of monarchies or presidents who died for their nations in order for their nations to progress.

If mere mortals find it hard to swallow, then imagine the God Status Yeshua Hamashiach was walking in, having to humble Himself to walk amongst the lost, sinful, suffering, and dying as the Light from Heaven in the world. Where He would Patiently demonstrate His Governments Power to heal and cast out sickness, infirmity and all types of demons including the forgiveness of sins.

This type of serving was so offensive to the religious poverty spirit that they plotted to end His life and even said let the iniquity of their murder on His life fall onto their children's children. The Spiritual Kingdom of Yeshua, The Door to Heaven, is still operating in automation thousands of years later. He's still transferring authority through Holy Spirit, the ministering angels, the same miracles in the bible and more are increasing with every generation.

As the world gets even darker, it's easier to fall into deception than ever before and as married couples in Covenant with Yeshua Hamashiach, as it gets darker and darker our Bridegroom Mysterion garments of righteousness will be manifested brighter and brighter. The divine condition will be serving one another without conditions, without limitations, and transcending serving each other fruit from the tree of good and evil (sin and death consciousness), to rather instead serve each other eternal fruit from the tree of Life (Unconditional Love, Eternal Life & Immortality).

John 17: 3 AMPC

3 And this is eternal life: [it means] to know (to perceive, recognize, become acquainted with, and understand) You, the only true *and* real God, and [likewise] to know Him, Jesus [as the] Christ (the Anointed One, the Messiah), Whom You have sent.

DOOR FOUR: BEING A FRIEND

John 15: 14 – 15 AMPC

14 You are My friends if you keep on doing the things which I command you to do. 15 I do not call you servants (slaves) any longer, for the servant does not know what his master is doing (working out). But I have called you My friends, because I have made known to you everything that I have heard from My Father. [I have revealed to you everything that I have learned from Him.]

What a privilege we have in Yeshua Hamashiach. This is what makes the Marriage Covenant and another gem of the Bridegroom Mysterion so exclusive. When we were going through pre-marital counseling in the foundation phase of our marriage, we were already good boyfriend and girlfriend five years deep. As we recall our backstory, we were way too much and more than the average friend zone….we were sinning against each other, but by His Grace! Yeshua let us into His secrets of marriage at the foundation phase, just after we were born again. We were good friends then, but now we are best of friends. In the Greek language, "Phileo" refers to brotherly and sisterly love. Yes! We have walked with Yeshua long enough to even learn about these revelations of the Bridegroom Mysterion.

The verse above explicitly exemplifies that He even says He doesn't let slaves (servants) know what He is doing. How often do we get a dream about something that is about to happen before it happens? How often do we fast and pray so we can prepare for the next season as a couple to make room in our hearts for God to direct our paths? How often do we keep secrets from each other as married couples?

These questions are a double-edged sword to us professing to be "Married in Christ", if God keeps no secrets from His friends, then how ought we be to keep our hearts open to enjoy each other's company in perpetual cycles of intimacy in Spirit, Soul, and Body? Yeshua, in the same passage, commands us to Love One Another with all of our being. We cannot cheat on Yeshua Hamashiach and think He never saw our secret, that's why spiritual blindness is so dangerous to our marriage ministries, because we can never cheat on our spouse and they would never know.

Their guardian angel, God The Father, Son, Holy Spirit, 7 Spirits of the Holy Spirit, Arch Angels, countless numerous angels and hosts, 24 Elders, 4 living Creatures, Cloud of Witnesses, Creation groaning!...meaning Heaven's Celestial and Earth's Terrestrial bodies are all watching...Lord be Gracious, help us discern with open spiritual eyes to see how wide and deep the roots and cosmic branches of God's friends are always abiding on our side.

Ephesians 5: 30 – 32 AMPC

30 Because we are members (parts) of His body. 31 For this reason a man shall leave his father and his mother and shall be joined to his wife, and the two shall become one flesh. 32 This mystery is very great, but I speak concerning [the relation of] Christ and the church.

DOOR FIVE: BEING A SON

Galatians 4: 1 – 6 KJV

[1] Now I say, That the heir, as long as he is a child, differs nothing from a servant, though he be lord of all; [2] But is under tutors and governors until the time appointed of the father. [3] Even so we, when we were children, were in bondage under the elements of the world: [4] But when the fullness of the time was come, God sent forth his Son, made of a woman, made under the law, [5] To redeem them that were under the law, that we might receive the adoption of sons. [6] And because ye are sons, God hath sent forth the Spirit of his Son into your hearts, crying, Abba, Father.

At this phase of our journey, we have the revelation that being a child is a phase of being parented, being a servant (slave) is also not the growth phase to settle for, because when parents leave, neither of them can exercise power to execute the title deeds and privileges because of a lack of maturity. In the Greek language elements translate to "stoicheia".

Sons and daughters are presented by Yeshua to the Father as mature citizens of the kingdom of God. They are not subject to the natural boundaries such as earth's gravity, water, air, and fire. These citizens experience the supernatural on a daily basis and discern that they are not from here but on assignment from the Kingdom of Heaven. Their spiritual passports are sons and daughters first by the Blood of Christ before they are just a number on their identity card and a barcode in the government database, a title name in their profession.

They have their spiritual senses exercised, and they walk by Faith and not by sight. They remember who they are and are conscious of their membership as Heavenly Kingdom Citizens of Love. They speak the language of Light and always seek the heart of the Father for all their moves.

They trust God, they are administrators of heavenly trust funds (The Blood) and distribute and carry the Spirit of Christ Yeshua Hamashiach in their Hearts. Wherever they go, they mediate with Christ to reconcile the relationship with humanity to their Father in Heaven. They are lovers of Peace and are able to bring the atmosphere over a nation under oppression into a supernatural state of Peace.

Matthew 5: 9 TLV

⁹ "Blessed are the peacemakers, for they shall be called sons of God.

Sons and Daughters are constantly living from the right hand of the Father in the Heavenly Places, and Holy Spirit-led encounters are a by-product of their visitations wherever they go. Sons and daughters are always seeking the Father's face. Yeshua Hamashiach, our Divine Brother (Phileo Lover) and Omni-Present God, also advocates for sons and presents them and invites them to fellowship with Him and The Father. Encounters with the heavenly beings and cloud of witnesses is not a foreign event.

Mark 9: 2-4 TLV

² After six days, *Yeshua* takes with Him Peter and Jacob and John, and brings them up a high mountain by themselves. And He was transfigured before them. ³ His clothes became radiant and brilliantly white, whiter than any launderer on earth could bleach them. ⁴ Then Elijah appeared to them with Moses, and they were talking with *Yeshua*.

Sons and daughters understand that without the Presence of God there is nothing that can be done. Without the daily bread from Heaven on Earth, the day was unproductive. They are constantly in fellowship with Yeshua and because he has become more than a friend to them they are presented to the Father as sons and daughters. They have a revelation of God as Father because the Son of God in their heart reveals the Divine Father to them as family and a spiritual function of Sovereignty.

Sons and Daughters are recognized by the angelic realm and when they pray God sends His highest ranking Angels to speak to them like Mary, Mother of Yeshua and Prophet Daniel who were

attended to by Arch Angel Gabriel. They pray and intercede for their nation's deliverance as a lifestyle, putting petitions for the nations above their own personal needs. Because The Father is pleased to see someone coming in agreement to decree and declare what is in Heaven to be on Earth, Father God sends His Arch Angels and army of hosts to provide protection and strategy for all including themselves.

John 5: 19 – 21 TLV

[19] Then Jesus answered and said to them, "Most assuredly, I say to you, the Son can do nothing of Himself, but what He sees the Father do; for whatever He does, the Son also does in like manner. [20] For the Father loves the Son, and shows Him all things that He Himself does; and He will show Him greater works than these, that you may marvel. [21] For as the Father raises the dead and gives life to *them,* even so the Son gives life to whom He will.

Sons and Daughters are focused on their inward appearance more than their outward appearance. We are dead to the world through the eternal bridge of the Bridegroom Mysterion, the Power of the Cross, Resurrection Power, and Eternal Life of Christ.

They know the Word of God is the doorway to the Heart of The Person of Christ and understand that there is no race, nor tribalism, titles, or gender in the spiritual realm, but acknowledge the feminine and masculine aspects of God are important and converge as One in Christ.

They discern that the kingdom of God is within us, and have understanding that it is not profitable to be an idol in this world, to be worshiped as a famous person and lose your soul. Sons and Daughters focus on fruit more than gifts of the spirit, they discern that the word "spirit" is equivalent to "angel" and without these angels there is no five fold ministry. Therefore, they will always give God the glory because their help comes from Father God, as administrators of Yeshua's Kingdom, they can authorize and dispatch the resources of Heaven's Kingdom on Earth.

Sons and Daughters are fulfilled by the divine intimate relationship, they discern that even the angels cannot fathom the great mystery of the Son and Father and the Spiritual Blood of Jesus, coursing through our spiritual veins from our Father, which is The True Light. The very Light that runs through our veins reflects His Limitless Fruit through us and thus resembles His imprinted image on us.

John 15: 1 - 5 TLV

15 "I am the true vine, and My Father is the gardener. 2 Every branch in Me that does not bear fruit, He takes away; and every branch that bears fruit, He trims so that it may bear more fruit. 3 You are already clean because of the word I have spoken to you. 4 Abide in Me, and I will abide in you. The branch cannot itself produce fruit, unless it abides on the vine. Likewise, you cannot produce fruit unless you abide in Me. 5 "I am the vine; you are the branches. The one who abides in Me, and I in him, bears much fruit; for apart from Me, you can do nothing.

DOOR SIX: BEING A BRIDE

Revelations 21:2 The Mirror

2 And I saw her, in spotless magnificence, the Holy City, the New Jerusalem, descending out of the heavens; having been fully prepared as a bride and beautifully adorned for her husband.

The Son of God, Yeshua, presents His Father's Sons/Daughters to become a Bride. This maturity stage of our spiritual growth is what we have termed the Butterflication Process. This is the climax of our relationship in the Spirit, Soul & Body. This is the mystical reunion within the heart of the Father, back into the eternal garden like Adam and Eve, translated to another dimension, be with YHWH like Enoch, building the family arch, and resting 40 days like Noah.

Cleaving and leaving from our forefathers to go into unknown terrain like Abraham, living through scarcity and plenty like Joseph, walking through the wilderness and unlearning Egypt in order to deliver our bloodlines like Moses, conquering the giants in the promised land like Joshua and Caleb, soaking in the anointing oils to prepare to meet the king like Esther.

Dancing naked and unashamed in Praise and Worship to God like David, Entering into the Holy of Holies into the bridal chamber to consummate and be enraptured by Mystical oneness in the Marriage bed like Solomon in song of songs, escaping the fires of hell like Shadrach, Meshach and Abednego, the lions den like Daniel and resurrecting from deep darkness and conquering death like Yeshua Hamashiach, Hallelujah!!!.......we can go for all eternity as I tap into the new wine enjoying all sorts of divine ecstasies.

The root word for orgasm in the Greek is translated "orgasmos" which means excitement. This is the realm of the Greek word "Eros" sensual and sexual desire, intense Love and Joy sustained from being rooted in drinking from the well of our youth. The book of Song of Songs, written by King Solomon, whose name translated means "Peace" expresses these ecstasies in poetic form, unveiling the multifold wisdom of the oneness of Marriage Covenant Passion in Christ.

This Bridegroom Mysterion is the limitless choirs composing songs upon songs, the diverse marriage ministries filling the Heavens and the Earth with testimonies of Love expressed through song. Each of us in Covenant Marriage in Christ are a unique song of songs, divine testimonies who demonstrate the fruitfulness, multiplication and dominion of our Heavenly Holy City on Earth.

We are the Bridegroom Mysterion, overcoming all the lying, stealing, and destructive schemes that are systematically designed to separate us from the Love of our Husband God.

Isaiah 54: 5 AMPC

5 For your Maker is your Husband—the Lord of hosts is His name—and the Holy One of Israel is your Redeemer; the God of the whole earth He is called.

We like the modern quantum physicist's terminology to describe the Quantum dimensions. Through revelations of the Cross of Christ, unknowingly and knowingly, we resonate with those "scientific terms" that we are all in a "quantum entanglement". A place where we are plugged into God's dimensions and integrated in time, space, matter, and beyond (spiritual realm)…where we explore how deep, how high, how long, and how wide the dimensions of the Government of the Cross of Christ, our eternal gateway into Unconditional Love is by Faith.

Ephesians 3: 17 - 19 AMPC

17 May Christ through your faith [actually] dwell (settle down, abide, make His permanent home) in your hearts! May you be rooted deep in love and founded securely on love, 18 That you may have the power and be strong to apprehend and grasp with all the saints [God's devoted people, the experience of that love] what is the breadth and length and height and depth [of it]; 19 [That you may really come] to know [practically, through experience for yourselves] the love of Christ, which far surpasses mere knowledge [without experience]; that you may be filled [through all your being] unto all the fullness of God [may have the richest measure of the divine Presence, and become a body wholly filled and flooded with God Himself]!

We die daily, and we live from the heavenly places in Christ, who strengthens us. Our Butterflication state of being keeps us in an ascended state of union with God, our Husband. We are unraveled as the Bridegroom Mysterion's rib, His wife and rib, His Bride...bone of my bone, flesh of my flesh, and spirit of my spirit. We multiply like Israel and the 12 tribes, we plant seeds that bear fruit after themselves (not like GMO seedless), on the third day we resurrect with Him from glory to glory. We cast a shadow across eternity with our rainbow glory wings, when they come together as the 7 Spirits of the Holy Spirit (spirit of the Lord, spirit of wisdom, spirit of understanding, spirit of counsel, spirit of might, spirit of knowledge, and the spirit of the fear of the Lord).

Yes! They do not mix into darkness as in the fallen colours of the earthly realm which manifest as absence of Light..... no! They make pure glory light and descend upon us as a glory light dove, a glory light slain sheep, a glory light horse with chariots and a bridal gown adorned with gemstones.

We live within the allegory of the Bridegroom, and we are always giving birth to Light, there is no night nor day in the Covenant Marriage, there is perpetual transfiguration in the divine rest day.

Isaiah 60:19 AMPC

[19] The sun shall no more be your light by day, nor for brightness shall the moon give light to you, but the Lord shall be to you an everlasting light, and your God your glory and your beauty.

Revelation 22: 4 - 5 AMPC

[4] They shall see His face, and His name shall be on their foreheads. [5] And there shall be no more night; they have no need for lamplight or sunlight, for the Lord God will illuminate them and be their light, and they shall reign [as kings] forever and ever (through the eternities of the eternities).

COUPLES OF THE BIBLE

We want to honour Apostle Johann Peter Melchizedek of the Cathedral of Glory. He is known to be an early mentor of the anointed man of God, Joseph Prince from Singapore, who first heard the deep revelation of the famous modern Grace message preached by Peter Tan before he was given the current name Johann Melchizedek Peter by the authority of YHWH Himself. Our thirst for knowing and learning about the deep mysteries of the Bride and the Bridegroom led us to him by Holy Spirit.

It is under this ministry where we first encountered the study of Soulmates in the bible and much more teaching, including the 7 Thunders prophecy. From this revelation of Soulmates the book, we have the permission to pen our revelations and have also done a video session online for the Couples Of The Bible. It is furthermore revelations and allegories that God has imparted to us by His divine Grace. We once again are eternally grateful because truly wisdom is better than choice gold and silver.

In summary, from the book Soulmate by Apostle Johann Peter Melchizedeck, he dives deep and shares about the following couples as soulmates:

Adam and Eve

Enoch, Noah, Shem and Giddel

Abraham and Sarah

Isaac and Rebekah

Jacob and Rachel

Joseph and Asenath

Moses and Zipporah

Boaz and Ruth

Aquila and Priscilla

He then unpacks the harmonization of the soulmates and how their dynamics to strike a balance worked in scripture because these are two individuals resonating at different frequencies to harmonize into a bandwidth that makes them one melody.

We resonate with all of them to a certain degree, and our favorite is the last couple, Aquila and Priscilla, which we learned have been important and being hospitable to Apostle Paul and Apostle Timothy in supporting the health of the Ephesus church in Rome. Under our organization, Lovelution Global Ministries, we have recorded and uploaded on YouTube the Couples Of The Bible Series, which was then birthed from identifying a need for couples to journey with us during COVID 19 Lockdown, as we looked into this study and rhema of Soulmates in the bible.

When we followed the stories of the family tree in the bible, Holy Spirit began to show us the pattern of the work of the kingdom of darkness and the life expectancy of people in the ancient biblical times and our modern times. We observed through revelation knowledge, how the deeper lying lines of the battle of souls over the human species were very strategic, and that there have always been two camps in the human species. Human beings who have traded their bloodlines to fallen angels to breed for the kingdom of darkness, and another group who have been a chosen gene, a generation of people who have kept their seed spotless and clean for the birth of the coming Messiah, Yeshua.

All along, the children of Israel have been seduced countless times to forfeit their divine birthright, to be a Holy Priesthood and preserve themselves as set apart for the giving birth of the Messiah.

The lifespan of Adam is recorded at 930 years, and we see now that by the time Moses is born, already children are being killed to prevent a liberator from Abraham's seed to free them from slavery. We see it again when Yeshua was born, that most children born at that time were being killed under Herod's command again.

Why was it so important to kill these babies? These wars are ancient and older than us, by the time one reads the Book of Revelation, John the Revelator speaks about seeing a pregnant queen who is pursued by a fiery-red dragon-like serpent, who tries to swallow the child before they are born. It is evident that we have entered a time of what Prophet Isaiah termed "deep darkness covers the earth". According to Guttmacher, an organization that has made an effort to follow the stats of abortion, it is recorded that:

- Unintended pregnancy and abortion are experiences shared by people around the world. These reproductive health outcomes occur irrespective of country income level, region or the legal status of abortion.

- Roughly 121 million unintended pregnancies occurred each year between 2015 and 2019.

- Of these unintended pregnancies, 61% ended in abortion. This translates to 73 million abortions per year.

Apostle Ed Silvoso from Argentina, the author of many books, including Anointed For Business, speaks in depth about Eliminating Systemic Poverty. Number 5 of the pivotal paradigms which are important to his organization, Transform Our World, is that "the premier social indicator that transformation has taken place is the elimination of systemic poverty". Any nation that lacks the capacity to raise responsible households and their children is a victim of systemic poverty.

The family nuclear structure, as this data shows, is a reflection of the life expectancy from the Adamic age, who lived 930 years, to 73 million plus wombs opting for abortion. Life expectancy and the marriage institution, as the first ministry since Adam and Eve is clearly under severe attack.

The kingdom of God suffers violence, and the violent take it by force. The New Creation Resurrection Life and Power of Yeshua is a necessary paradigm shift. It is clear that when the Glory of the Lord rises upon those who will embrace the New Creation reality, the Kingdom of God and His righteousness will bring perfect alignment with those who walk by Faith and all things under the King's authority will be really added to them.

There is an odd couple in the bible where King Ahab and Jezebel (The daughter of Baal) were married. She introduced the worship of an idol, Baal, which was a foreign god and enemy to YHWH. Israel's prophets were further persecuted and ordered to be killed as they fled for their lives including Prophet Elijah. It is important to study this matter further and when looking into the opposing spirits and how they affected the nation of Israel in the natural, one will note that there was a famine with no rain for a season, and YHWH had given Elijah authority for it not to rain until repentance comes.

How we perceive marriage from ancient times and how we raise our children in these end times is important as the Body of Christ. When will we begin to perceive the beginning times (new Jerusalem and new earth) if we are struggling to discern beyond the elementary problems as a society, where such sensitive matters have been normalized?

We are challenged and burdened as The Body of Christ and believe truly God is brooding over the planet for signs, miracles, and wonders because only an act of God will deliver us from systemic poverty. Covenant Marriage is being restored, and families are being blessed in the Body of Christ to steward divine mysteries. The nations are coming to our light and kings to the brightness of your rising.

The New Creation, divine family bloodline of Yeshua Hamashiach, has been given Eternal Life to live it now and not later. We are calling and are called to shout out like wisdom to married couples from Mount Zion and those who are joining us now and in the near future to walk in Victory.

Praying that all who have read this book may be blessed and exceedingly empowered by our story and know that God is our Husband in Covenant Marriage and will never allow us to be separated from His Love. If God is on our side, who can be against us? We are Victorious in Yeshua's name.

[31] What then shall we say to these things? If God is for us, who can be against us? [32] He who did not spare His own Son, but delivered Him up for us all, how shall He not with Him also freely give us all things? [33] Who shall bring a charge against God's elect? It is God who justifies. [34] Who is he who condemns? It is Christ who died, and furthermore is also risen, who is even at the right hand of God, who also makes intercession for us. [35] Who shall separate us from the love of Christ? Shall tribulation, or distress, or persecution, or famine, or nakedness, or peril, or sword? [36] As it is written:

"For Your sake we are killed all day long;

We are accounted as sheep for the slaughter."

[37] Yet in all these things we are more than conquerors through Him who loved us. [38] For I am persuaded that neither death nor life, nor angels nor principalities nor powers, nor things present nor things to come,

[39] nor height nor depth, nor any other created thing, shall be able to separate us from the love of God which is in Christ Jesus our Lord.

This is our Love testimony and story with Jesus Christ, the lover of our souls. He has held us by His Grace and held our hands unconditionally, leading us through the desert where we have been refined by His holy fire. Living on manna whilst dying from self, being pruned to produce this fruit offering of covenant Love. Having our scales peeled off through long suffering and to help those facing extreme difficulty in marriage, that...there is nothing impossible or too hard for God! We love you and are looking forward to hearing and sharing your unique stories in the eternal now.

Hebrews 7 : 22 The Mirror

22 **Melchizedeck mirrors Christ in the highest office of priesthood mediator between God and mankind. Jesus is now the living proof of God's covenant pledge to benefit mankind in a far better way than under any previous arrangement.**

Yours Faithfully,

Legae and Nomatamsanqa Sebakwane
bride of the Bridegroom

In the Order of Melchizedek

Amen

References:

Soulmates of the bible

© Copyright 2018 by Johann Melchizedek Peter

ABOUT THE AUTHORS

Legae and Nomatamsanqa Sebakwane are the founders of Lovelution Global Ministries, which is a marriage coaching institution with partnerships spanning across the globe.

To book our marriage coaching sessions email:
lovelutionglobal@gmail.com

Take your free TEAM ME Couples Profile Tool:
http://teamme.com/bridegroom

Seraph Creative is a collective of artists, writers, theologians & illustrators who desire to see the body of Christ grow into full maturity, walking in their inheritance as Sons of God on the Earth.

Sign up to our newsletter to know about future exciting releases.

Visit our website: www.seraphcreative.org

www.ingramcontent.com/pod-product-compliance
Lightning Source LLC
Chambersburg PA
CBHW050008040726
47599CB00014B/1268